Satyavan

The Golden Tower & The Future of the Earth

Pravir Malik, Ph.D.

Copyright © 2026 Pravir Malik
All rights reserved.

ISBN-13: 979-8-9943369-0-8

Published by *Possibilities Publishing*
San Francisco, USA

"For ever love, O beautiful slave of God!
O lasso of my rapture's widening noose,
Become my cord of universal love.
The spirit ensnared by thee force to delight
Of creation's oneness sweet and fathomless,
Compelled to embrace my myriad unities
And all my endless forms and divine souls.
O Mind, grow full of the eternal peace;
O Word, cry out the immortal litany:
Built is the golden tower, the flame-child born."

(Sri Aurobindo, *Savitri*)

Table of Contents

INTRODUCTION	5
CHAPTER 1: EARTH'S FLOWERING	16
CHAPTER 2: THE LORD OF LIFE	20
CHAPTER 3: DEATH'S TREMENDOUS HOUR	25
CHAPTER 4: THE CHANGING SOUL OF THE WORLD	32
CHAPTER 5: FOURFOLD GROWTH OF EARTH	37
CHAPTER 6: VISHNU'S NARAD	40
CHAPTER 7: THE BLUE-THROATED ASCETIC	47
CHAPTER 8: DYUMATSENA'S LINEAGE	51
CHAPTER 9: THE TRIPLE HOLY MARRIAGE	54
CHAPTER 10: THE TERRESTRIAL LABOR	60
CHAPTER 11: THE DOUBLE TWILIGHT	72
CHAPTER 12: EARTH'S SAVITRI	76
CHAPTER 13: SAVITRI'S DAWN	87
CHAPTER 14: FOURFOLD DAWNS	93
CHAPTER 15: AWAKENING THE SUPERMAN	98
CHAPTER 16: IMMORTALITY AND MAGIC ORDER	109
CHAPTER 17: THE SUPRAMENTAL WORLD	118
CHAPTER 18: PSYCHIC BEING'S MATERIALIZATION	128
CHAPTER 19: THE GODS AWAKE	134
CHAPTER 20: HIGH TRUTH'S FEET	145
A CONTEMPLATIVE MAP OF EARTH'S EVOLUTION	153

Introduction

In the Author's Note to *Savitri*, Sri Aurobindo states that "Satyavan is the soul carrying the divine truth of being within itself but descended into the grip of death and ignorance."

It is helpful to read the full note before embarking on a deeper contemplation of Satyavan:

"The tale of Satyavan and Savitri is recited in the Mahabharata as a story of conjugal love conquering death. But this legend is, as shown by many features of the human tale, one of the many symbolic myths of the Vedic cycle. Satyavan is the soul carrying the divine truth of being within itself but descended into the grip of death and ignorance; Savitri is the Divine Word, daughter of the Sun, goddess of the supreme Truth who comes down and is born to save; Aswapati, the Lord of the Horse, her human father, is the Lord of Tapasya, the concentrated energy of spiritual endeavour that helps us to rise from the mortal to the immortal planes; Dyumatsena, Lord of the Shining Hosts, father of Satyavan, is the Divine Mind here fallen blind, losing its celestial kingdom of vision, and through that loss its kingdom of glory. Still this is not a mere allegory, the characters are not personified qualities, but incarnations or emanations of living and conscious Forces with whom we can enter into concrete touch and they take human bodies in order to help man and show him the way from his mortal state to a divine consciousness and immortal life."

In the *Agenda* (January 22, 1961) the Mother states about the relationship between Savitri and Satyavan:

"The entire last part, from the moment she goes to seek Satyavan in the realm of Death, the whole description of what happens there, right up to the end, where every possible offer is made to tempt her, everything she must refuse to continue her terrestrial labor... it is my experience EXACTLY.

Savitri is really a condensation, a concentration of the universal Mother—the eternal universal Mother, Mother of all universes from all eternity—in an earthly personality for the Earth's salvation. And Satyavan is the soul of the Earth, the Earth's jiva. So when the Lord says, 'he whom you love and whom you have chosen,' it means the earth.

He says that she very carefully takes the SOUL of Satyavan into her arms, like a little child, to pass through all the realms and come back down to earth.

He hasn't forgotten a single detail to make it easy to understand—for someone who knows how to understand. And it is when Savitri reaches the earth that Satyavan regains his full human stature."

In 1953 Questions & Answers (CWM, 9 December 1953) in response to a question about Savitri, The Mother reveals:

"Savitri represents the Mother's Consciousness, doesn't she?

Yes."

And further, to the question about Satyavan:

"What does Satyavan represent?

Well, he is the Avatar. He is the incarnation of the Supreme."

Yet, when we first encounter Satyavan in the first canto (Pg 10, C I: *The Symbol Dawn*, Bk I: *The Book of Beginnings*), it is by way of an enigmatic line: "This was the day when Satyavan must die." In fact, the phrase 'Satyavan must die' is repeated 4 times in

Savitri, with the three other utterances expressed by Narad in *The Book of Fate*:

1. "This day returning Satyavan must die" (Pg 431, C I: *The Word of Fate*, Bk VI: *The Book of Fate*)
2. "It is decreed and Satyavan must die" (Pg 458, C II: *The Way of Fate and the Problem of Pain*, Bk VI: *The Book of Fate*)
3. "In vain thou mournst that Satyavan must die" (Pg 459, C II: *The Way of Fate and the Problem of Pain*, Bk VI: *The Book of Fate*)

Satyavan, as we have learnt, is the soul carrying the divine truth of being within itself but descended into the grip of death and ignorance. He is mentioned about 80 times in *Savitri*, and even though the tale is titled *Savitri*, it is equally about Satyavan, Savitri's 'other self'. The tale can be seen from the point of view of Satyavan. He is there in the very first canto, and in the the very last. The long-standing debate that is taking place in Savitri's flaming heart is between the ancient disputants – Earth, and Love, and Doom. They have been there from time immemorial, those godheads who have arisen from the Inconscient (Pp 9 – 10, C I: *The Symbol Dawn*, BK I: *The Book of Beginnings*):

"All came back to her: Earth and Love and Doom,
The ancient disputants, encircled her
Like giant figures wrestling in the night:
The godheads from the dim Inconscient born
Awoke to struggle and the pang divine,
And in the shadow of her flaming heart,
At the sombre centre of the dire debate,
A guardian of the unconsoled abyss
Inheriting the long agony of the globe,
A stone-still figure of high and godlike Pain
Stared into Space with fixed regardless eyes
That saw grief's timeless depths but not life's goal."

"This was the day that Satyavan must die." That is the last line of the very first canto. Already encircling Savitri we have met Earth and Love and Doom. And the Mother has said that Satyavan is the soul of the earth. This we will uncover in greater detail as we journey through this exploration. But here he is, a cryptic figure, and we have been told that he must die. But clearly it is not earth that is dying when he dies, even though he is the soul of the earth. And already we have heard in this very canto, *The Symbol Dawn*, of a "significant myth Telling of a greatness of spiritual dawns," one in which the very first line of *Savitri* states "It was the hour before the Gods awake."

So Satyavan's death that must happen, must be related to the significant myth telling of a greatness of spiritual dawns, where the Gods will awake. Satyavan must die, for the Gods to awake. Right now it was the hour before They awake. Not a millennia, not an eon, but an hour.

Beyond this first mention of Satyavan in the first canto, stating that he must die, the second mention of him does not occur until page 392, in the second canto, *Satyavan* in *The Book of Love*. Yet there is a build up and context of the change that earth and its inhabitants need to go through.

In the *Book of the Traveler of the Worlds*, we follow Aswapati's journey into all the realms that influence earth and influence earth nature. Soon after he embarks on the world-stair, a compendium of all the planes that influence earth dynamics, he entered the Life plane replete with all its glories such as the 'double majesty' when Life is throned with mind. There was 'happiness great and grave', action was tinged with dream, and there was a childlike mirth and joy, and work was play and play the only work (Pg 126, Canto III: *The Glory and Fall of Life*, Bk II: *The Book of the Traveler of the Worlds*).

Meanwhile there was a call from earth. Life heard the call and went on her way to offer her gifts:

"But while the magic breath was on its way,
Before her gifts could reach our prisoned hearts,
A dark ambiguous presence questioned all.
The secret Will that robes itself with Night
And offers to spirit the ordeal of the flesh,
Imposed a mystic mask of death and pain."
(Pg 130, Canto III: *The Glory and Fall of Life*, Bk II: *The Book of the Traveler of the Worlds*)

Aswapati now continues his journey through the worlds of life, and before reaching the planes of mind, enters into the world of night, and then into the world of falsehood. There he sees the origin of the dark ambiguous presence that questions all:

"But from the Night another answer came.
A seed was in that nether matrix cast,
A dumb unprobed husk of perverted truth,
A cell of an insentient infinite."
(Pg 222, Canto VIII: *The World of Falsehood*, Bk II: *The Book of the Traveler of the Worlds*)

These give great insight into the obstacles that have held back the journeying of the earth towards the destination hinted at in *The Symbol Dawn*. Aswapati's quest for a power that can decisively change the dynamics of earth so that 'The huge foreboding mind of Night' (Pg 1, C 1: *The Symbol Dawn*, Bk I: *The Book of Beginnings*) can be overcome, takes him into the planes of mind, into the world-soul where we learn more about the soul of the world that is Satyavan, into the kingdoms of the greater knowledge, into the house of the Spirit, before he finally has audience with The Divine Mother.

Book II, *The Book of the Traveler of the Worlds*, gives insight into the dynamics alive on earth and the change that must come, of which the death of Satyavan is absolutely required. But it is the death of the origin of these dynamics or that configure the dynamics of the world that relates to the necessary death of Satyavan. He has to become something different. So the soul of the world takes an evolutionary leap and for that Savitri, his 'other self' (Pg 366, C II: *The Growth of the Flame*, Book IV: *The Book of Birth and Quest*), is the master executor.

The evolutionary leap is perhaps summarized by the line "Built is the golden tower, the flame-child born" (Pg 702, *The Soul's Choice and the Supreme Consummation*, Bk XI: *The Book of Everlasting Day*). Satyavan represents the 'golden tower', that which connects material or bodily possibility to the golden light, while Savitri frames the 'flame-child', a new genre of psychic being that holds a a more powerful flame and possibility for the emergence of future beings, including the supramental being, than has ever existed before.

The building of the golden tower, as also the birth of the flame-child, means that the foundation of earth's future evolutionary changes has been set in place. There is now a leap, foretold by *The Symbol Dawn* and in the greater dawn nursed in Savitri's bosom (Pg 724, *The Return to Earth*, Book XII: *Epilogue*). Outpourings of that continuing dawn are glimpsed in *Vision and the Boon* and in *The Everlasting Day*.

This book is a series of connected explorations suggesting how the earth changes and will continue to change through a changing Satyavan:

- In *Chapter 1* we begin with *Earth's Flowering* that contrasts the earth at the beginning of *Savitri*, with that at its end, and in the context of Satyavan as the soul of the earth.
- In *Chapter 2* we then contemplate the *The Lord of Life*, highlighting the protagonist of the mysterious play, Aswapati, who has mastered all the inner worlds on the world-stair, changed their dynamics, created the seeds of a new creation, and received the boon of Savitri from the

Divine Mother, thereby setting into motion all that will change the future of the earth.

- *Chapter 3, Death's Tremendous Hour,* centers around what this tremendous hour may mean, while also discussing the fragmentation due to Death, its conquest leading to Knowledge, which in the cosmic scheme of things is a prerequisite for the action of Love.
- *Chapter 4, Changing Soul of the World,* emphasizes that the soul of the world is not static, as is clear from the very first canto which concludes with the line, "This is the day that Satyavan must die." We also know from Savitri's conquest of Death and in the subsequent return of Satyavan with Savitri to earth, that it is a different Satyavan that has returned. This chapter explores what such a changing soul of the world may mean in the context of the two-in-one and the Power that brought them forth.
- *Chapter 5, Fourfold Growth of Earth,* suggests, by a concise macro-analysis of the architecture implicit in *Savitri*, how the world will change. The macro-analysis is conducted by applying the functions of the Vedic Solar Kings – Varuna, Aryaman, Mitra, and Bhaga – to *Savitri*.
- Such change is a cosmic necessity and *Chapter 6, Vishnu's Narad,* explores how the cosmic stamp carried by the sage from Paradise must influence the balance between remaining in the status quo and decisively moving forward. Narad also sheds insight into the nature of Satyavan.
- Change has to be endured and *Chapter 7, Blue-Throated Ascetic,* highlights the holding of such equilibrium and the tremendous change that is going to happen when Savitri meets Satyavan. There is solemnity to the place where the first satisfied plan exists, highlighted by the figures of the blue-throated ascetic, Durga, and the fallen Divine Mind. Being the meeting place of Satyavan and Savitri, the place where Savitri performs her yoga prior to the world-changing inner journey, it will also become the

place where the Divine Mind regains sight, and where Krishna and Kali descend to earth with the luminous Savitri and Satyavan.

- *Chapter 8, Dyumatsena's Lineage,* discusses the dynamic tension between the 'mind of Night' and the 'Divine Mind' so that the next necessary status in Satyavan's evolution can be reached. He has to be close to this tension and intimate with it to develop the discriminative power to continue to choose the inevitable future demanded by the immortal litany that announces the building of the golden tower and the birth of the flame-child.

- *Chapter 9, Triple Holy Marriage,* points to the conquests to be made for the holy marriage between the eternal Lord and Spouse to be achieved, and for the divine family to be born. Already the marriage has occurred twice. But it is at the third time, once luminous Savitri and Satyavan return to earth, that it becomes fruitful.

- *Chapter 10, Terrestrial Labor,* provides insight on the multiple lines of the Divine, usually in the form of vibhutis who often act simultaneously to bring about the evolution of the earth. Sri Aurobindo points out that recording such action would mean writing all of history, while the Mother points out that all of written history would need to be rewritten to be truly accurate.

- *Chapter 11, Double Twilight,* highlights two twilights. These occur due to Savitri's yoga culminating in her also mastering the secret of World-personality. She is going to change the order of the walk where the mortal leads and the god and spirit follow, with her the leader, still behind. The first twilight has to do with Death transitioning to the figure of the fourfold AUM. The second has to do with the shift of a cyclically unfulfilled earth toward a foundation of fulfillment.

- *Chapter 12, Earth's Savitri,* suggests how Savitri's earth, the chosen place of her work, has now been changed so that Savitri has become earth's Savitri. There has been a fundamental change to the soul of the earth, so that it becomes possible for Savitri to be earth's Savitri. In 'earth's Savitri' there is 'illimitable change': power too great, a bliss too large, a light too intense, love too boundless, as though these things can only be – and in a way that has never been before - because it is in the matter of the earth that it is happening.

- *Chapter 13, Savitri's Dawn*, highlights the decisive time that has come, and the 'greater dawn' that Savitri nurses in her bosom, unlike any other that has preceded it. When she returns to earth, the result is Satyavan in his full human stature, the golden tower, that can now also see freely and far, become the flame-child, and be the ground on which all future dawns shall be established. The epic *Savitri* itself appears to be only the very beginning of *Savitri's Dawn* hinted at in the first half of *The Symbol Dawn*. We have to turn to other parts of *Savitri* to get a sense for what this continuing dawn may mean.

- *Chapter 14, Fourfold Dawns,* describes further dawns influenced by Maheshwari, Mahakali, Mahasaraswati, and Mahalakshmi. These fourfold dawns appear imminent, if not already on-going, and points too, to the greater dawns that require that the fourfold powers of the Mother be grounded and active. As suggested in Sri Aurobindo's, The Mother – "Only when the Four have founded their harmony and freedom of movement in the transformed mind and life and body, can those other rarer Powers manifest in the earth movement and the supramental action become possible."

- *Chapter 15, Awakening the Superman,* explores the waking of the superman in mortal man. The prerequisites of the 'Mighty Mother' taking birth in Time, and God being born into the human clay lead inevitability to this. The only question is to what degree has this awakening already taken place?

- *Chapter 16, Magic Order,* discusses immortality of the being that must bring about a new magic order beyond that of the mechanical universe. Such immortality may also be a spur for the formation of a 'conscious entity' at the level of the cells, that then allows the body also to remember God. This then is a prerequisite for physical immortality.
- In *Chapter 17, The Supramental World,* the Mother shares the fact that the supramental world already exists, that she is permanently there in a supramental body, and that what needs to be done is that an intermediate zone between the physical world and the supramental world needs to be built. She describes the experience of a huge ship where this is being done.
- *Chapter 18, Psychic Being's Materialization*, further explores the connection between the psychic fire, psychic being, the flame-child, the golden tower, and the supramental being. As Mother reveals, the psychic being becomes the supramental being. Is the flame-child, then, the same thing as the supramental being? If the flame-child is born from a particular kind of psychic fire, one that has become from the kind of tapasya and love as shown by Savitri, then perhaps this is the case.
- *Chapter 19, The Gods Awake,* explores some facets of gods and Gods in light of Savitri's opening line: "It was the hour before the Gods awake". The supramental world is already born and will progressively become materially more real. It is suggested that the holding of a different flame that allows the birth of the flame-child, a being that does not require sheaths of ignorance but instead is cased in the safety of the supramental substance, would allow the Gods to awake.
- *Chapter 20, High Truth's Fee*t, explores the establishment of high Truth, requiring mastery of the mechanism that facilitates the constant flipping to a lesser reality. Satyavan, the soul of the earth, the golden tower, holds new statuses animated by the flame-child to

stabilize intermediate races, until Sri Aurobindo himself arrives in the first supramental body built in the supramental way, engendering even brighter rays in Savitri's continuing Dawn.

Chapter 1: Earth's Flowering

In *The Debate of Love and Death* (Pg 637, CIII, Bk X: *The Book of the Double Twilight*) Savitri tells Death: "Thy Gifts resist. Earth cannot flower if lonely I return."

For earth to flower, she must return with Satyavan, the soul of the earth who is the incarnation of the Supreme. It is he that through the ages has held the evolutionary changes in the climbing from becoming to becoming interned in the being-possibilities involved in matter.

Mother sheds light on the formation of the earth (*CWM, Vol. 04: Q&A 1951*, 24 March):

"The formation of the earth as we know it, this infinitesimal point in the immense universe, was made precisely in order to concentrate the effort of transformation upon one point; it is like a symbolic point created in the universe to make it possible, while working directly upon one point, to radiate it over the entire universe.

If we want to make the problem a little more comprehensible, it is enough to limit ourselves to the creation and the history of the earth, for it is a good symbol of universal history.

From the astronomical point of view the earth is nothing, it is a very small accident. From the spiritual point of view, it is a symbolic willed formation. And as I have already said, it is only upon earth that this Presence is found, this direct contact with the supreme Origin, this presence of the divine Consciousness hidden in all things.

The other worlds have been organised more or less hierarchically, if one may say so, but the earth has a special formation due to the direct intervention, without any intermediary, of the supreme Consciousness in the Inconscient.

...

(Mother answering a question to do with beings of the other worlds and planets having a psychic being). No, it is a purely terrestrial phenomenon. Only, there is nothing against the idea that psychic beings may go to the other worlds if it so pleases them. There is no reason to think that one cannot, if one went to another planet, meet psychic beings; it is not impossible; but these would be psychic beings formed upon earth who have become free in their movement, going here and there at will for some reason or other. All knowledge in all traditions, from every part of the earth, says that the psychic formation is a terrestrial formation and that the growth of the psychic being is something that takes place upon earth. But once they are formed and free in their movement, they can go anywhere in the universe, they are not limited in their movement; but their formation and growth belong to the terrestrial life, for reasons of concentration."

She also sheds light on the formation of the earth in the context of *Savitri* in the Agenda (Vol. 02, 1961, July 28):

"Let's take *Savitri*, which is very explicit on this: the universal Mother is universally present and at work in the universe, but the earth is where concrete form is given to all the work to be done to bring evolution to its perfection, its goal. Well, at first there's a sort of emanation representative of the universal Mother, which is always on earth to help it prepare itself; then, when the preparation is complete, the universal Mother herself will descend upon earth to finish her work. And this She does with Satyavan—Satyavan is the soul of the earth. She lives in close union with the soul of the earth and together they do the work; She has chosen the soul of the earth for her work, saying, 'HERE is where I will do my work.'"

So if Savitri were to return to the earth without Satyavan, in the absence of its soul, the earth would become a hierarchical world like any other in the universe, and the possibility of Love continuing to manifest would be stalled. Death then would continue to reign as the supreme power over all life.

The contrast of the earth, where Satyavan exists as a human strongly influenced by the 'mind of Night' and the luminous Satyavan returned to earth and now existing in his full human stature, where in effect he is the golden-tower, can be seen by examining some of the differences between the earth as described in the very first canto of *Savitri*, *The Symbol Dawn*, and the very last canto, *The Return to Earth*, where the holy marriage between the eternal Lord and Spouse has been fulfilled by him returning hand in hand with her. While these are taken up subsequently in the book, here some of these differences will be highlighted.

The earth in *The Symbol Dawn* is a 'green smiling dangerous world'. Giant figures are wrestling in the night, and 'at the sombre centre of the dire debate' exists a figure of 'godlike Pain' that sees only 'grief's timeless depths':

"All came back to her: Earth and Love and Doom,
The ancient disputants, encircled her
Like giant figures wrestling in the night:
The godheads from the dim Inconscient born
Awoke to struggle and the pang divine,
And in the shadow of her flaming heart,
At the sombre centre of the dire debate,
A guardian of the unconsoled abyss
Inheriting the long agony of the globe,
A stone-still figure of high and godlike Pain
Stared into Space with fixed regardless eyes
That saw grief's timeless depths but not life's goal."
(Pp 9-10, C I: *The Symbol Dawn*, Bk I: *The Book of Beginnings*)

By contrast in *The Return to Earth*, Savitri, following some questions by Satyavan, reveals:

"All now is changed, yet all is still the same.
Lo, we have looked upon the face of God,
Our life has opened with divinity.
We have borne identity with the Supreme
And known his meaning in our mortal lives.
Our love has grown greater by that mighty touch
And learned its heavenly significance,
Yet nothing is lost of mortal love's delight.
Heaven's touch fulfils but cancels not our earth…"
(Pg 719, C I: *The Return to Earth*, Bk XII: *Epilogue*)

The question is, what has led to this change? To begin to understand this we first contemplate Aswapati, The Lord of Life.

Chapter 2: The Lord of Life

It has been said that Aswapati, the great Lord of Tapasya, the Lord of the Horse, the Lord of Life, represents the figure of Sri Aurobindo. The Mother has said about Sri Aurobindo (*CWM, Words of the Mother – I*, 30 March 1914): "What Sri Aurobindo represents in the history of the earth's spiritual progress is not a teaching, not even a revelation; it is a mighty action straight from the Supreme."

We must assume then, that in Books I (*The Book of Beginnings*), II (*The Book of the Traveller of the Worlds*), and III (*The Book of the Divine Mother*), when we read about the journeying of Aswapati, we are hearing something about Sri Aurobindo himself, and some of the actions that he concerned himself with while in the physical body. For those who love Sri Aurobindo, *Savitri* then, assumes an extraordinary significance. To see further that in his becoming the Lord of Life, one who has mastered all the inner worlds on the world-stair, changed their dynamics, created the seeds of a new creation, and received the boon of Savitri from the Divine Mother, he has set into motion all that will change the entire future of the earth, is to begin to partake of that future in a special way. Just as Savitri herself was initiated into a first yoga by the words of Aswapati, and then into a far more significant second yoga through the words of Narad, the words of Sri Aurobindo's *Savitri* initiate us into the great adventure of beginning to understand who Savitri and Satyavan are, and into becoming the adventurers journeying toward that glorious destiny that awaits us.

When Aswapati is first introduced it is as the 'Protagonist of the mysterious play'. After he has met the Divine Mother in Book III, *The Book of The Divine Mother*, and returned to earth, it is as 'The Lord of Life'. It is in this protagonist becoming the Lord of Life, that the master lever initiating the building of the golden tower and the birth of the flame-child is set into motion, assuring finally that a greater dawn will be housed in Savitri's bosom.

We meet Aswapati, the 'protagonist of the mysterious play' in Bk 1, CIII (Pp 22-3, CIII: *The Yoga of the King: The Yoga of the Soul's Release*, Bk I: *The Book of Beginnings*) who brings down her radiant power to the earth.

"A WORLD'S desire compelled her mortal birth.
One in the front of the immemorial quest,
Protagonist of the mysterious play
In which the Unknown pursues himself through forms
And limits his eternity by the hours
And the blind Void struggles to live and see,
A thinker and toiler in the ideal's air,
Brought down to earth's dumb need her radiant power."

We see glimpses of his yoga through three cantos in Book 1. At the culmination he has gained freedom from individual and cosmic bonds and numerous siddhis, and can attend to the problem of this creation by first breaking into another Space and Time (Pg 91, CV: *The Yoga of the King: The Yoga of the Spirit's Freedom and Greatness*, Bk I: *The Book of Beginnings*):

"Affranchised from the net of earthly sense
Calm continents of potency were glimpsed;
Homelands of beauty shut to human eyes,
Half-seen at first through wonder's gleaming lids,
Surprised the vision with felicity;
Sunbelts of knowledge, moonbelts of delight
Stretched out in an ecstasy of widenesses
Beyond our indigent corporeal range.
There he could enter, there awhile abide.
A voyager upon uncharted routes
Fronting the viewless danger of the Unknown,
Adventuring across enormous realms,
He broke into another Space and Time."

He now proceeds to explore the World-Stair (Bk II, C I). Along the way he sees how glorious Life is in its own plane, and how when it answers to the deep need of the awakening gods on material earth, by bringing its gifts, 'the secret Will that robes itself with Night' transformed it and instead 'Imposed a mystic mask of death and pain' (Pg 130, C III: *The Glory and Fall of Life*, Bk II: *The Book of the Traveller of the Worlds*):

"But while the magic breath was on its way,
Before her gifts could reach our prisoned hearts,
A dark ambiguous Presence questioned all.
The secret Will that robes itself with Night
And offers to spirit the ordeal of the flesh,
Imposed a mystic mask of death and pain.
Interned now in the slow and suffering years
Sojourns the winged and wonderful wayfarer
And can no more recall her happier state,
But must obey the inert Inconscient's law,
Insensible foundation of a world
In which blind limits are on beauty laid
And sorrow and joy as struggling comrades live."

But Aswapati wants to penetrate far more deeply into the secret Will that robes itself with Night to discover the root of the other answer that had emerged from it (Pg 222, *The World of Falsehood, The Mother of Evil and the Sons of Darkness*, Bk II: *The Book of the Traveller of the Worlds*):

"When nothing was save Matter without soul
And a spiritless hollow was the heart of Time,
Then Life first touched the insensible Abyss;
Awaking the stark Void to hope and grief
Her pallid beam smote the unfathomed Night
In which God hid himself from his own view.
In all things she sought their slumbering mystic truth,
The unspoken Word that inspires unconscious forms;

She groped in his deeps for an invisible Law,
Fumbled in the dim subconscient for his mind
And strove to find a way for spirit to be.
But from the Night another answer came.
A seed was in that nether matrix cast,
A dumb unprobed husk of perverted truth,
A cell of an insentient infinite.
A monstrous birth prepared its cosmic form
In Nature's titan embryo, Ignorance."

We can see that Aswapati leaves no leaf unturned. Just as he has penetrated into the darkest depths, so too he ascends into the highest heights. But beyond that too, by his power he often changes the reality of the planes he enters. Thus, having entered into this world of the mother of evil and the sons of darkness, by his own power he tears the formats of Hell. He emerges into the *Paradise of the Life-Gods* (Bk 2 C IX), and then continues to the planes of Mind. He has still not found the power: that power that can address the fundamental question that he is concerned with – that of changing the trajectory of possibility so that God himself can build His resplendent Kingdom in matter.

He proceeds onto the *World-Soul* (Bk 2 C XIV), sees how there are deeper possibilities that inform it – the deathless Two-in-One – that will change the status and dynamis of that soul, and continues to the *Kingdoms of Greater Knowledge*. He now has to tear out of himself the very influence that exists in him, due to being born a material being. He, the Master of Yoga, and a direct action from the Supreme, now seeds a new creation. This is his prerogative. Only he can do it and he creates the kernel of a new world (Pp 322-3, C III: *The House of the Spirit and the New Creation*, Bk III: *The Book of the Divine Mother*):

"Then suddenly there came a downward look.
As if a sea exploring its own depths,
A living Oneness widened at its core
And joined him to unnumbered multitudes.

A Bliss, a Light, a Power, a flame-white Love
Caught all into a sole immense embrace;
Existence found its truth on Oneness' breast
And each became the self and space of all.
The great world-rhythms were heart-beats of one Soul,
To feel was a flame-discovery of God,
All mind was a single harp of many strings,
All life a song of many meeting lives;
For worlds were many, but the Self was one.
This knowledge now was made a cosmos' seed:
This seed was cased in the safety of the Light,
It needed not a sheath of Ignorance.
Then from the trance of that tremendous clasp
And from the throbbings of that single Heart
And from the naked Spirit's victory
A new and marvellous creation rose."

He has done almost all he can, and is ready now to meet the Divine Mother, where one more task remains. For only she can make that seed cased in the safety of light and the new and marvelous creation materially real.

Chapter 3: Death's Tremendous Hour

We are led now into the passage packed with prophecy. There is a revealing interchange between Aswapati and the Divine Mother, where the journeys of man, and of Aswapati, and the origins of Savitri, are put in context, and the boon in response to Aswapati who is carrying the world's desire with him - its dumb need that even it is not aware of - is granted (Pg 346, C IV: *The Vision and the Boon*, Bk III: *The Book of the Divine Mother*):

"O strong forerunner, I have heard thy cry.
One shall descend and break the iron Law,
Change Nature's doom by the lone spirit's power."

She who shall descend is further described by the Divine Mother:

"A limitless Mind that can contain the world,
A sweet and violent heart of ardent calms
Moved by the passions of the gods shall come.
All mights and greatnesses shall join in her;
Beauty shall walk celestial on the earth,
Delight shall sleep in the cloud-net of her hair,
And in her body as on his homing tree
Immortal Love shall beat his glorious wings.
A music of griefless things shall weave her charm;
The harps of the Perfect shall attune her voice,
The streams of Heaven shall murmur in her laugh,
Her lips shall be the honeycombs of God,
Her limbs his golden jars of ecstasy,
Her breasts the rapture-flowers of Paradise.
She shall bear Wisdom in her voiceless bosom,
Strength shall be with her like a conqueror's sword
And from her eyes the Eternal's bliss shall gaze."
(Pg 346, C IV: *The Vision and the Boon*, Bk III: *The Book of the Divine Mother*)

And than She utters the astounding prophesy:

"A seed shall be sown in Death's tremendous hour,
A branch of heaven transplant to human soil;
Nature shall overleap her mortal step;
Fate shall be changed by an unchanging will."
(Pg 346, C IV: *The Vision and the Boon*, Bk III: *The Book of the Divine Mother*)

Particularly the last lines in this boon 'A seed shall be sown in Death's tremendous hour, A branch of heaven transplant to human soil;' remain mysterious. The 'seed' perhaps is the seed that Aswapati created that has been cased in the safety of the light, which requires 'an unchanging will' – the will of Savitri - to 'transplant to human soil;'. But what is 'Death's tremendous hour'? Is this the hour where finally Death is defeated by Savitri – licked by light?:

"Although he knew refusing still to know,
Although he saw refusing still to see.
Unshakable he stood claiming his right.
His spirit bowed; his will obeyed the law
Of its own nature binding even on Gods.
The Two opposed each other face to face.
His being like a huge fort of darkness towered;
Around it her light grew, an ocean's siege.
Awhile the Shade survived defying heaven:
Assailing in front, oppressing from above,
A concrete mass of conscious power, he bore
The tyranny of her divine desire.
A pressure of intolerable force
Weighed on his unbowed head and stubborn breast;
Light like a burning tongue licked up his thoughts,
Light was a luminous torture in his heart,
Light coursed, a splendid agony, through his nerves;
His darkness muttered perishing in her blaze.
Her mastering Word commanded every limb

And left no room for his enormous will
That seemed pushed out into some helpless space
And could no more re-enter but left him void."
(Pg 667, C IV: *The Dream Twilight of the Earthly Real*, Bk X: *The Book of the Double Twilight*)

Death even calls to Night and the Inconscient from which he was born, and than is eaten by light:

"He called to Night but she fell shuddering back,
He called to Hell but sullenly it retired:
He turned to the Inconscient for support,
From which he was born, his vast sustaining self;
It drew him back towards boundless vacancy
As if by himself to swallow up himself:
He called to his strength, but it refused his call.
His body was eaten by light, his spirit devoured.
At last he knew defeat inevitable
And left crumbling the shape that he had worn,
Abandoning hope to make man's soul his prey
And force to be mortal the immortal spirit."
(Pg 667, C IV: *The Dream Twilight of the Earthly Real*, Bk X: *The Book of the Double Twilight*)

Or is it referring to the even more cryptic and perhaps autobiographical reference in one of Sri Aurobindo's final edits (https://thewindsofwonder.org/2024/09/18/in-savitri-the-last-three-passages-dictated-by-sri-aurobindo/) to *Savitri* just weeks before his passing? (Pg 445, C II: *The Way of Fate and the Problem of Pain*, Bk VI: *The Book of Fate*):

"He who has found his identity with God
Pays with the body's death his soul's vast light.
His knowledge immortal triumphs by his death."

If the latter, then it must be that 'His knowledge immortal' has forever changed the fragmented knowledge that drives Night,

Hell, and the Inconscient, depriving them of their dark status and dynamis of being. The Mother states that supramental force of a material nature passed from Sri Aurobindo's body into hers at the time of his passing (*CWM, Vol. 11: Notes on the Way*, 20 December 1972):

"He had gathered in his body a great amount of supramental force and as soon as he left... You see, he was lying on his bed, I stood by his side, and in a way altogether concrete—concrete with such a strong sensation as to make one think that it could be seen—all this supramental force which was in him passed from his body into mine. And I felt the friction of the passage. It was extraordinary—extraordinary. It was an extraordinary experience. For a long time, a long time like that (Mother indicates the passing of the Force into her body). I was standing beside his bed, and that continued.

Almost a sensation—it was a material sensation.

For a long time."

She materially, and he occultly, must have caused his knowledge, immortal, to triumph by his death. Or perhaps in the process of death he forever changes something in it, and is it that that is referred to as 'Death's tremendous hour'?

Now, to put this in context – that is, what is the significance of Sri Aurobindo's birth, here is a passage from Mother's Collected Works (4 September 1957, *CWM - Questions and Answers - 1957 - Volume 6*, pp.178 – 179):

"Today I received a question about a phrase I used on the fourteenth of August, the eve of Sri Aurobindo's birthday. And this question seemed interesting to me because it was about one of those rather cryptic phrases, that are almost ambiguous through simplification, and which was intended to be like that, so that each one might understand it according to his own plane of consciousness. I have already spoken to you several times of this possibility of understanding the same words on different planes; and these words were intentionally expressed with a simplification, a deliberate vagueness, precisely so that they would serve as a vehicle for the complexity of meaning they had to express.

This meaning is a little different on the different planes, but it is complementary, and it is only really complete when one is able to understand it on all these planes at once. True understanding is a simultaneous understanding in which all the meanings are perceived, grasped, understood at the same time; but to express them, as we have a very poor language at our disposal, we are obliged to say them one after another, with many words and many explanations.... That's what I am going to do now.

The question is about the phrase in which I spoke of the birth of Sri Aurobindo—it was on the eve of his birthday—and I called it an "eternal birth". I am asked what I meant by "eternal".

Of course, if the words are taken literally, an "eternal birth" doesn't signify much. But I am going to explain to you how there can be—and in fact is—a physical explanation or understanding, a mental understanding, a psychic understanding and a spiritual understanding.

Physically, it means that the consequences of this birth will last as long as the Earth. The consequences of Sri Aurobindo's birth will be felt throughout the entire existence of the Earth. And so I called it "eternal", a little poetically.

Mentally, it is a birth the memory of which will last eternally. Through the ages Sri Aurobindo's birth will be remembered, with all the consequences it has had.

Psychically, it is a birth which will recur eternally, from age to age, in the history of the universe. This birth is a manifestation which takes place periodically, from age to age, in the history of the Earth. That is, the birth itself is renewed, repeated, reproduced, bringing every time perhaps something more—something more complete and more perfect—but it is the same movement of descent, of manifestation, of birth in an earthly body.

And finally, from the purely spiritual point of view, it could be said that it is the birth of the Eternal on Earth. For each time the Avatar takes a physical form it is the birth of the Eternal himself on Earth.

All that, contained in two words: "eternal birth".

So, to conclude, I advise you, in future, before telling yourself: "Why! What does this mean? I don't understand it at all; perhaps it is not expressed properly," you could say to yourself: "Perhaps I am not on the plane where I would be able to understand", and try to find behind the words something more than mere words. There.

I think this will be a good subject for our meditation.

(Meditation)"

Now, referring to the line 'His knowledge immortal triumphs by his death,' in an entry in *Mother's Agenda* (Vol 7, April 16, 1966) there is further insight into the necessity of Knowledge reigning before Love can manifest:

'"...And finally one loves purely and simply without any other need or joy than that of loving."
That, to me, according to my personal experience, is really omnipotence.

It's a power than can achieve anything—anything at all. Nothing is impossible to it.

But I have also carefully observed that if "that" manifested indiscriminately, as it were, if it came as something that imposed itself in the earth atmosphere without control or discernment, it would be... All that denies that Power (denies it wittingly or unwittingly) would be as though annulled. So the outward, apparent consequences would be... too awesome. That's what Sri Aurobindo wrote; he said Knowledge must come first. Truth must reign before Love can manifest massively—*a wholesale manifestation.*

Now it's filtered, as it were. It is still filtered.

But the vibratory quality of "that" is truly something beyond all imagination. Diseases, difficulties... none of it has any reality.

The body constantly used to ask (not a sign or an assurance or a proof: it's all of that together), it used to ask for a sort of sensation (sensation, if it can be called that) that "it is the Lord that rules" (I am putting it in childlike words because they are the truest), that it is the Lord that rules. It asked for "that" all the time, the way a child could ask: "that" in all the innumerable nothings one does all the time, which are the very fabric of the body's existence. It became so intense.... Anything perceived as separate from "that" becomes inert: ashes. Inert without even the power of inertia: the inertia of dust. I mean that a rock has a power in its existence, a power of cohesion, of duration—it's not even that: it's dust. So then, there was constantly, constantly that prayer in the body. And that's what led me to the experience.

When "that" is there, everything seems to swell with a golden, luminous, radiating Power: it's so intense as to have volume!... If that isn't there, everything is dust.

So, naturally, there is constantly in all the cells the aspiration, the intense will for there to remain nothing but That.'

Chapter 4: The Changing Soul of the World

We know that the soul of the world is not static. This is clear from the very first canto which concludes with the line, "This is the day that Satyavan must die." We also know from Savitri's conquest of Death in the canto *The Dream Twilight of the Earthly Real* (Canto IV, Bk X: *The Book of the Double Twilight*), and the subsequent return of Satyavan with Savitri in *The Return to Earth* (Book XII: *Epilogue*), that it is a different Satyavan who has returned. In several parts of *Savitri*, Satyavan is referred to as the soul of the world: "Release the soul of the world called Satyavan" (Pg 666 Canto IV: *The Dream Twilight of the Earthly Real*, Bk X: *The Book of the Double Twilight*), and further the changing nature of this world soul is reinforced by lines such as:

"He is my soul that climbs from nescient Night,
Through life and mind and supernature's Vast,
To the supernal light of Timelessness
And my eternity hid in moving Time
And my boundlessness cut by the curve of Space."
(Pp 702-703, C I: *The Soul's Choice and the Supreme Consummation*, Bk XI: *The Book of Everlasting Day*).

But what does such a changing soul mean? We see a glimpse of this in *The World Soul* (pg 295, Canto XIV, Bk II: *The Book of the Traveller of the Worlds*) as Aswapati travels into the depths of the World Soul. Behind the apparent reality is the figure of the deathless Two-in-One whose trance of bliss sustained the world…

"…To the source of all things human and divine.
There he beheld in their mighty union's poise
The figure of the deathless Two-in-One,
A single being in two bodies clasped,
A diarchy of two united souls,
Seated absorbed in deep creative joy;
Their trance of bliss sustained the mobile world."

This deathless Two-in-One must relate to Savitri and her other or second self, Satyavan. Why would they be referred to as each other's 'other' (Pg 366, *The Growth of the Flame*; Pg 686, *The Souls Choice & The Supreme Consummation*) or 'second' self (Pg 374, *Call to the Quest*), and why would the Supreme refer to them as the 'dual power' (Pg 702, 705) in *The Book of Everlasting Day* if in fact they were not two-in-one?

Savitri's first yoga, that unlike other yoga has her search the world and in the process make it her own, is initiated by Aswapati, the Lord of Life, in the canto *The Call to the Quest*. Perhaps also it is fitting that a yoga of this nature where discovery is by way of an external rather an internal process would be initiated by one who has also become the Lord of Life:

"O spirit, traveller of eternity,
Who cam'st from the immortal spaces here
Armed for the splendid hazard of thy life
To set thy conquering foot on Chance and Time,
The moon shut in her halo dreams like thee.
A mighty Presence still defends thy frame.
Perhaps the heavens guard thee for some great soul,
Thy fate, thy work are kept somewhere afar."
(Pp 373-74, C III: *The Call to the Quest*, Bk IV: *The Book of Birth and Quest*)

Aswapati continues, also drawing attention to the fact that her other self, Satyavan, the soul of the earth, will greaten his life with a message written with the Eternal's sun-white script. This implies also that the soul of the world will be greatened with Savitri's own heavenly strength and bliss:

"Thy spirit came not down a star alone.
O living inscription of the beauty of love
Missalled in aureate virginity,
What message of heavenly strength and bliss in thee

33

Is written with the Eternal's sun-white script,
One shall discover and greaten with it his life
To whom thou loosenest thy heart's jewelled strings."
(Pg 374, ClII: *The Call to the Quest*, Bk IV: *The Book of Birth and Quest*)

And now Aswapati issues the divine command:

"O rubies of silence, lips from which there stole
Low laughter, music of tranquillity,
Star-lustrous eyes awake in sweet large night
And limbs like fine-linked poems made of gold
Stanzaed to glimmering curves by artist gods,
Depart where love and destiny call your charm.
Venture through the deep world to find thy mate.
For somewhere on the longing breast of earth,
Thy unknown lover waits for thee the unknown."
(Pg 374, ClII: *The Call to the Quest*, Bk IV: *The Book of Birth and Quest*)

He states that Savitri needs no other guide than the One within her:

"Thy soul has strength and needs no other guide
Than One who burns within thy bosom's powers."
(Pg 374, ClII: *The Call to the Quest*, Bk IV: *The Book of Birth and Quest*)

And here Aswapati refers to Savitri's 'second self', reinforcing the notion of the 'Two-in-One', stating that 'hand in hand' they will 'confront Heaven's question, Life':

"There shall draw near to meet thy approaching steps
The second self for whom thy nature asks,
He who shall walk until thy body's end
A close-bound traveller pacing with thy pace,
The lyrist of thy soul's most intimate chords

Who shall give voice to what in thee is mute.
Then shall you grow like vibrant kindred harps,
One in the beats of difference and delight,
Responsive in divine and equal strains,
Discovering new notes of the eternal theme.
One force shall be your mover and your guide,
One light shall be around you and within;
Hand in strong hand confront Heaven's question, life:
Challenge the ordeal of the immense disguise.
Ascend from Nature to divinity's heights;
Face the high gods, crowned with felicity,
Then meet a greater god, thy self beyond Time."
(Pp 374-5, CIII: The Call to the Quest, Bk IV: The Book of Birth and Quest)

It is none other than the Divine Mother who has brought the deathless Two-in-One forth:

"Behind them in a morning dusk One stood
Who brought them forth from the Unknowable.
Ever disguised she awaits the seeking spirit;
Watcher on the supreme unreachable peaks,
Guide of the traveller of the unseen paths,
She guards the austere approach to the Alone."
(pg 295, Canto XIV: The World Soul, Bk II: The Book of the Traveller of the Worlds)

And the notion of this source of change that clearly also implies that the world soul will continue to change:

"At the beginning of each far-spread plane
Pervading with her power the cosmic suns
She reigns, inspirer of its multiple works
And thinker of the symbol of its scene.
Above them all she stands supporting all,
The sole omnipotent Goddess ever-veiled
Of whom the world is the inscrutable mask;

The ages are the footfalls of her tread,
Their happenings the figure of her thoughts,
And all creation is her endless act."
(Pg 295, Canto XIV: *The World Soul*, Bk II: *The Book of the Traveller of the Worlds*)

Chapter 5: Fourfold Growth of Earth

As the soul of the world changes, we have a glimpse for what this means at the micro level in the canto *The Vision and the Boon* (Bk III: *The Book of the Divine Mother*), and this will be taken up in more detail in the exploration on *Fourfold Dawns* later in this book. In the meanwhile though it is useful to consider such change from the macro perspective as intimated by the architecture of *Savitri* itself. For this we turn to Sri Aurobindo's insights in *The Secret of the Veda*.

In the Rig-Veda the Solar Kings, Sons of Aditi, The Divine Mother, are referred to as Varuna, Mitra, Aryaman, and Bhaga. The extent to which their essential natures are made active in the dynamics of the world, further invokes a downpour of the corresponding parts of Aditi – Mahasaraswati, Maheshwari, Mahakali, and Mahalakshmi respectively, to change the very 'symbols of her scenes', 'her inscrutable mask', 'her tread on the ages', all happenings, and creation itself, so that something more of the deathless Two-in-One is bought forward to also change the nature of the world soul.

In *The Book of the Traveller of the Worlds*, Aswapati first encounters 'The World Stair'. And here one gets the sense that it is related to what is described in the section about Varuna in *Secret of the Veda*:

"In the vast, where there is no foundation, Varuna has built a high pyramid of the fuel of sacrifice for the fire that must be the blazing material of a divine Sun….The Path is a constant making and building of new truth, new powers, higher realizations, new worlds. All heights to which we can climb from the basis of our physical existence are described in the symbolic figure as mountain summits upon the earth and Varuna of the vision holds them all in himself. World after world is reached as level and ever higher level of a great mountain; the voyager in the forward march of Varuna is said to to lay his grasp on all things that are born in all the statuses. But his highest goal must be the highest triple world of the Deva." (Pg 455, *The Guardians of the Light, The Secret of the Veda*).

But no higher world can be reached without sacrifice so that the dynamics of lower worlds no longer has sway on the traveler. And so in successfully traveling the World Stair, thereby changing the active dynamics in the world, it must be that Aditi's aspect of Mahasaraswati is further invoked to change the corresponding pillar of the world soul.

The travel itself though requires the aspiration and power of Aryaman, and with this happening so that world after world is crossed, it must be that Aditi's aspect of Mahakali is invoked to change the corresponding pillar of the world soul. We see this same dynamic in the yoga of Savitri as detailed in Book 7, *The Book of Yoga*, where she move from realization to realization, as she readies herself for her imminent encounter with Death.

Conquest by knowledge is a key theme in *Savitri*, and this allows the right harmony of Mitra to thereby arrange things. For this harmony is founded on the overcoming of that which constrains – the very 'mind of Night' referred to in the third line of the epic. By Death being conquered, first in the hidden worlds on The World Stair, and then by Savitri conquering Death, the basis of the cosmic restrictive knowledge is overcome, and then correspondingly the harmony of Mitra allows Aditi's aspect of Maheshwari to begin to change that aspect of the world soul.

Finally, in *The Book of the Everlasting Day*, the basis and destiny of bliss is initiated, when the dynamics of Bhaga become active. "Bhaga is Savitri the Creator, he who brings forth from the unmanifest Divine the truth of a divine universe, dispelling from us the evil dream of this lower consciousness in which we falter amidst a confused tangle of truth and falsehood, strength and weakness, joy and suffering. An infinite being delivered out of imprisoning limits, and infinite knowledge and strength receiving in thought and working out in will a divine Truth, an infinite beatitude possessing and enjoying all without division, fault or sin, this is the creation of Bhaga Savitri, this that greatest Delight." (Pg 464, *The Guardians of the Light, The Secret of the Veda*). As this dynamic becomes more active than it must be that Aditi's aspect of Mahalakshmi further changes the corresponding aspect of the world soul.

"Thus in the divine creation of the fourfold Savitri founded on Varuna, combined and guided by Mitra, achieved by Aryaman, enjoyed in Bhaga: Aditi the infinite Mother realizes herself in the human being by the birth and works of her glorious children." (Pg 464, *The Guardians of the Light, The Secret of the Veda*).

This is a prophesy and the destiny of the world. The soul of the world, Satyavan, will go through progressive changes. But already that has begun. And the promise of it being further expedited made clear with the descent also of Krishna and Kali with Savitri, as she returns to earth with Satyavan, after her encounter with the Supreme in his abodes of the everlasting day, as will be taken up in *Earth's Savitri*.

Chapter 6: Vishnu's Narad

The question is, why does Narad need to show up in *Savitri*. After all, we already have three Avatars in *Savitri*. As described in the *Authors Note* to *Savitri*, there is Aswapati, 'Lord of the Horse, the Lord of Tapasya, whose concentrated energy of spiritual endeavour helps us to rise from the moral to the immortal planes'. We have Savitri, 'the Divine Word, daughter of the Sun, goddess of the supreme Truth who comes down and is born to save'. We have Satyavan, 'the Soul, carrying the divine truth of being within itself but descended into the grip of death and ignorance'.

This perhaps is made clearer in the passage where Narad is first introduced at the beginning of *The Book of Fate*. He is the extraordinary 'heavenly sage from Paradise'. This passage begins with 'He passed from Mind into material things' through a process of what appears to be materialization as the poet describes a passage through ether, Air, Fire, sap, and Matter (Pp 415-16, Cl: *The Word of Fate*, Bk 6: *The Book of Fate*):

"Below him circling burned the myriad suns:
He bore the ripples of the etheric sea;
A primal Air brought the first joy of touch;
A secret Spirit drew its mighty breath
Contracting and expanding this huge world
In its formidable circuit through the Void;
The secret might of the creative Fire
Displayed its triple power to build and form,
Its infinitesimal wave-sparks' weaving dance,
Its nebulous units grounding shape and mass,
Magic foundation and pattern of a world,
Its radiance bursting into the light of stars;
He felt a sap of life, a sap of death;
Into solid Matter's dense communion
Plunging and its obscure oneness of forms

He shared with a dumb Spirit identity."

His spiritual stature and occult mastery is also made clear by these lines.

"He shared with a dumb Spirit identity.
He beheld the cosmic Being at his task,
His eyes measured the spaces, gauged the depths,
His inner gaze the movements of the soul,
He saw the eternal labour of the Gods,
And looked upon the life of beasts and men."
(Pg 416, C I: *The Word of Fate*, Bk VI: *The Book of Fate*)

It seems that Paradise is keenly interested in the affairs of this creation. While the work is already going on through the presence of three Avatars, yet what is about to occur on earth is no trivial matter. This has been foreseen, and Narad's coming here makes clear the cosmic importance of the action that is about to take place. In some sense all the future destiny of the cosmos must depend on it. Paradise too is going to play its part in the creation of the 'divine Event'.

The context of his visit is made clearer in these lines:

"He sang no more of Light that never wanes,
And oneness and pure everlasting bliss,
He sang no more the deathless heart of Love,
His chant was a hymn of Ignorance and Fate."
(Pg 416, C I: *The Word of Fate*, Bk VI: *The Book of Fate*)

But further, there is a relationship between Narad and Vishnu, and in his chant he continues:

"He sang the name of Vishnu and the birth
And joy and passion of the mystic world,
And how the stars were made and life began

And the mute regions stirred with the throb of a Soul."
(Pg 416, C I: *The Word of Fate*, Bk VI: *The Book of Fate*)

But clearly Narad is not here to ensure that what Vishnu has already done in terms of his incarnations as past avatars continues to exist. As the ambassador of Vishnu he perhaps is more concerned with ensuring the fruition of the future dynamics of his Guru.

In *Secret of the Veda*, Sri Aurobindo refers to the 'future mighty Triad': "...Vishnu, Rudra, Brahmanaspati, the future mighty Triad, preside over the indispensable conditions, - for the one paces out the vast framework of the inner worlds in which our soul-action takes place, the other in his wrath and might and violent beneficence forces onward the great evolution and smites the opponent and the recusant and the ill-doer, and the third administers always the seed of the creative word from the profundities of the soul..." (Pg 491).

The 'hour before the Gods awake' must be drawing near for we see the action of the future mighty Triad in *Savitri*. In Aswapati's travels through the worlds (Bk II: *The Book of the Traveller of the Worlds*) we see how he has altered the framework of the inner worlds by creating a new cosmos' seed from a which a new and marvelous creation arose, in addition to his tearing the formats of Hell, and altering the reality of several other inner worlds. This is clearly the action of Vishnu. In *The Vision and the Boon* (BK III: *The Book of the Divine Mother*) Aswapati relates his vision in which 'A giant dance of Shiva tore the past', which is the action of Rudra. In *The Eternal Day: The Soul's Choice and the Supreme Consummation* (Bk XI: *The Book of Everlasting Day*) the following lines indicate the action of Brahmanaspati administering the seed of the creative word from the profundities of the soul (Pg 702):

"O Word, cry out the immortal litany:
Built is the golden tower, the flame-child born."

Narad arrives at King Aswapati's palace just as Savitri returns from her quest and has married Satyavan. Savitri had performed a yoga, initiated by Aswapati, to find her other self. Now there is another yoga, one that results in the conquest of Death, that Narad initiates her into with his cry:

"Then cried the sage piercing the mother's heart,
Forcing to steel the will of Savitri,
His words set free the spring of cosmic Fate.
The great Gods use the pain of human hearts
As a sharp axe to hew their cosmic road:
They squander lavishly men's blood and tears
For a moment's purpose in their fateful work."
(Pg 429, C I: *The Word of Fate*, Bk VI: *The Book of Fate*)

He continues, describing aspects of Satyavan:

"A living knot of golden Paradise,
A blue Immense he leans to the longing world,
Time's joy borrowed out of eternity,
A star of splendour or a rose of bliss.
In him soul and Nature, equal Presences,
Balance and fuse in a wide harmony."
(Pg 416, C I: *The Word of Fate*, Bk VI: *The Book of Fate*)

Is this 'living knot of golden Paradise' the same Paradise as Narad's Paradise? If Satyavan is the avatar of the Supreme then this must be possible. There must be some deeper relationship between Vishnu as one of the future Triad, who will be established as Gods of the cosmos, and the necessity of the transformation of Satyavan due to the material convergence with his other self, Savitri.

The rarity of this being, and the necessity of Satyavan's death is further reinforced as Narad continues:

"His strength is like a tower built to reach heaven,

A godhead quarried from the stones of life.
O loss, if death into its elements
Of which his gracious envelope was built,
Shatter this vase before it breathes its sweets,
As if earth could not keep too long from heaven
A treasure thus unique loaned by the gods,
A being so rare, of so divine a make!
In one brief year when this bright hour flies back
And perches careless on a branch of Time,
This sovereign glory ends heaven lent to earth,
This splendour vanishes from the mortals' sky:
Heaven's greatness came but was too great to stay.
Twelver swift-winged months are given to him and her,
This day returning Satyavan must die."
(Pg 431, C I: *The Word of Fate*, Bk VI: *The Book of Fate*)

Narad's reference to Satyavan as 'a godhead quarried from the stones of life' and 'his strength is like a tower built to reach heaven' also sets up the notion arrived at later, that the 'golden tower' referred to later is none other than the future Satyavan.

The Author has called this book, the book where Narad arrives, *The Book of Fate*. And it is in dialog with the 'Queen-browed' human mother of Savitri, and Aswapati that the balance in Fate is revealed. The Cosmic stamp carried by the sage from Paradise must influence this balance. While the two Avatars are clearly on one end of the scale, the queen-mother 'Lending her speech to the surface soul on earth' (pg 437) must represent the heavy weight on the other side.   Satyavan at this point appears to be in the middle of this cosmic scale. In the normal course of things it would be:

"As if earth could not keep too long from heaven
A treasure thus unique loaned from the gods"
(Pg 431, C I: *The Word of Fate*, Bk VI: *The Book of Fate*)

This treasure, Satyavan, is the soul of Earth, and equally Earth could remain where it is, or it could move toward the side of the scale with Aswapati and Savitri.

As the Mother says in the *Agenda* (January 22, 1961): 'Savitri is really a condensation, a concentration of the universal Mother—the eternal universal Mother, Mother of all universes from all eternity—in an earthly personality for the Earth's salvation. And Satyavan is the soul of the Earth, the Earth's jiva.' And Narad has come to steel the will of Savitri. It is in one brief year that Satyavan must die:

"In one brief year when this bright hour flies back
And perches careless on a branch of Time,
This sovereign glory ends heaven lent to earth,
This splendour vanishes from the mortal's sky:
Heaven's greatness came, but was too great to stay.
Twelve swift-winged months are given to him and her;
This day returning Satyavan must die."
(Pg 431, C I: *The Word of Fate*, Bk VI: *The Book of Fate*)

The variabilities in fate, of moving toward one end of the scale or another, is reinforced by the notion of 'a branch of Time'. The carelessness of the surface soul of earth would push it toward one outcome and the Earth would continue in that way. But there is another branch of Time that is possible, and becomes inevitable by the forcing to steel the will of Savitri.

'Fate is Truth working out in Ignorance' (pg 458), and the arrival of Narad is the stamp from Paradise wanting that Truth to work out faster in the Ignorance. What Savitri does and can bear will alter the outcome of Fate:

"My will is part of the eternal Will,
My fate is what my spirit's strength can make,
My fate is what my spirit's strength can bear;"
(Pg 435, CI: *The Word of Fate*, Bk 6: *The Book of Fate*)

In a letter to a disciple the Avataric demand on humanity is reinforced by Sri Aurobindo (CWSA Vol 36, *Autobiographical Notes*):

"But we are the pioneers hewing our way through the jungle of the lower prakriti. It will not do for us to be cowards and shirkers and refuse the burden, to clamour for everything to be made quick and easy for us. Above all I demand from you endurance, firmness, heroism, - the true spiritual heroism. I want strong men, I do not want emotional children."

In the lineage of Savitri and Satyavan we also see the mixture of influences suggesting part of what each will face. Savitri's mother, the queen who can lend her speech to the surface soul of earth, suggests to Savitri to walk the measured middle way. Satyavan's father is the 'Divine Mind here fallen blind, losing its celestial kingdom of vision, and through that loss its kingdom of glory.' The Divine Mind has been subdued by the 'mind of Night', and it is in the soul of the Earth advancing to another equilibrium of being, that the Divine Mind can regain its kingdom of glory.

Chapter 7: The Blue-Throated Ascetic

There are several ways to understand who Satyavan is. One is by tracing the journey that Savitri makes to find her second self. She goes through villages, and cities, and palaces, and hermitages, meeting a cross-section of humanity – scholars, leaders, warriors, sages – and still finds him not. She has traversed the best of humanity and then comes to a place where the blue-throated ascetic, with his vast extended spirit, chooses not to escape into some vast void or brahman, but instead stays in the world swallowing its poison. The ascetic must be playing a role helping to maintain the world's equilibrium.

In fact the holding of such an equilibrium is a necessity when change is going to happen. Some beings have to be able to maintain the balance through an astounding display of endurance. Then can change more safely happen. And there is tremendous change that is going to happen when Savitri meets Satyavan. All is waiting for this and Gods will only awake in matter once the possibility inherent in the meeting of Savitri and Satyavan has been fulfilled.

Still, this – the blue-throated ascetic - is not he, not Satyavan. But this, where the blue-throated ascetic abides, is the destined meeting place of Satyavan and Savitri:

"At the end reclined a stern and giant tract
Of tangled depths and solemn questioning hills,
Peaks like a bare austerity of the soul,
Armoured, remote and desolately grand
Like the thought-screened infinities that lie
Behind the rapt smile of the Almighty's dance."
(Pg 390, C I: *The Destined Meeting-Place*, Bk V: *The Book of Love*)

And the 'forest matted-head' where Nature resonates with the Shiva-power:

"A matted forest-head invaded heaven
As if a blue-throated ascetic peered
From the stone fastness of his mountain cell
Regarding the brief gladness of the days;
His vast extended spirit couched behind.
A mighty murmur of immense retreat
Besieged the ear, a sad and limitless call
As of a soul retiring from the world."
(Pp 390-1, C I: *The Destined Meeting-Place*, Bk V: *The Book of Love*)

Further emphasized is the sadness adorned with a brief felicitous hour, where the sacrificant, Savitri, will meet Love:

"This was the scene which the ambiguous Mother
Had chosen for her brief felicitous hour;
Here in this solitude far from the world
Her part she began in the world's joy and strife.
Here were disclosed to her the mystic courts,
The lurking doors of beauty and surprise,
The wings that murmur in the golden house,
The temple of sweetness and the fiery aisle.
A stranger on the sorrowful roads of Time,
Immortal under the yoke of death and fate,
A sacrificant of the bliss and pain of the spheres,
Love in the wilderness met Savitri."
(Pp 391, C I: The Destined Meeting-Place, Bk V: The Book of Love)

This place also has other formidable gods and undertones that influence it. First of all this was where 'The Mighty Mother lay outstretched at ease' (Pg 390) and 'All was in line with her first satisfied plan.":

"Magician of her rapt felicities,
Blithe, sensuous-hearted, careless and divine,
Life ran or hid in her delightful rooms;

Behind all brooded Nature's grandiose calm.
Primaeval peace was there and in its bosom
Held undisturbed the strife of bird and beast.
Man the deep-browed artificer had not come
To lay his hand on happy inconscient things,
Thought was not there nor the measurer, strong-eyed toil,
Life had not learned its discord with its aim.
The Mighty Mother lay outstretched at ease.
All was in line with her first satisfied plan;
Moved by a universal will of joy
The trees bloomed in their green felicity
And the wild children brooded not on pain."

The Mighty Mother is at ease. Primaeval peace was in this place and Life had not learned its discord with its aim. Perhaps it is in such area that the beginnings of a second satisfied plan begins. Perhaps the first satisfied plan has created an occult rhythm of sorts in which here too the next satisfied plan will begin to emerge. For we find that in *The Return to Earth* everything is different though yet the same.

This is the place where also Durga receives the prayer uttered by Savitri, as suggested by the line 'What prayer she breathed her soul and Durga knew' in the canto *Death in the Forest* (Pg 561, Canto Three: *Death in the Forest*, Book VIII: *The Book of Death*) before her encounter with Death:

"Then silently she rose and, service done,
Bowed down to the great goddess simply carved
By Satyavan upon a forest stone.
What prayer she breathed her soul and Durga knew.
Perhaps she felt in the dim forest huge
The infinite Mother watching over her child,
Perhaps the shrouded Voice spoke some still word."

It is also the place where the fallen King (Pg 424, Canto I: *The Word of Fate*, Book VI: *The Book of Fate*) has been exiled:

"Father and king, I have carried out thy will.
One whom I sought I found in distant lands;
I have obeyed my heart, I have heard its call.
On the borders of a dreaming wilderness
Mid Shalwa's giant hills and brooding woods
In his thatched hermitage Dyumatsena dwells,
Blind, exiled, outcast, once a mighty king."

As Sri Aurobindo states in the Author's Note: "Dyumatsena, Lord of the Shining Hosts, father of Satyavan, is the Divine Mind here fallen blind, losing its celestial kingdom of vision, and through that loss its kingdom of glory."

Hence, we have the solemnity of the place where the first satisfied plan exists, highlighted by the figures of the blue-throated ascetic, Durga, and the fallen Divine Mind. Through becoming the meeting place of Satyavan and Savitri, and the place where Savitri performs her yoga before embarking on the world-changing inner journey, it will also become the place where the Divine Mind regains sight, as we see in *The Return to Earth* (Book XII: Epilogue), and where Krishna and Kali descend to earth with the luminous Savitri and Satyavan (Pg 711, C I: *The Eternal Day: The Soul's Choice and the Supreme Consummation*, Bk XI: *The Book of Everlasting Day*).

Chapter 8: Dyumatsena's Lineage

Sri Aurobindo, in the Author's Note to *Savitri*, states about Dyumatsena: "Dyumatsena, Lord of the Shining Hosts, father of Satyavan, is the Divine Mind here fallen blind, losing its celestial kingdom of vision, and through that loss its kingdom of glory."

On Page 403, in Canto III: *Satyavan and Savitri*, Book V: *The Book of Love*, in one of Satyavan's replies to Savitri he says:

"In days when yet his sight looked clear on life,
King Dyumatsena once, the Shalwa, reigned
Through all the tract which from behind these tops
Passing its days of emerald delight
In trusting converse with the traveller winds
Turns, looking back towards the southern heavens,
And leans its flank upon the musing hills.
But equal Fate removed her covering hand.
A living night enclosed the strong man's paths,
Heaven's brilliant gods recalled their careless gifts,
Took from blank eyes their glad and helping ray
And led the uncertain goddess from his side.
Outcast from empire of the outer light,
Lost to the comradeship of seeing men,
He sojourns in two solitudes, within
And in the solemn rustle of the woods."

Is this a sacrifice? A sacrifice of the Divine Mind, participating here in the great adventure and the promise of 'a significant myth' in which there is 'a greatness of spiritual dawns'? (Pg 4, Canto I: *The Symbol Dawn*, Bk I: *The Book of Beginnings*). Like Life that journeyed to earth 'And strove to find a way for spirit to be' receiving instead another answer from Night (pg 222, C VIII: *The World of Falsehood*, Book II: *The Book of the Traveler of the Worlds*), in which 'Life grew into a huge and hungry death' (pg 223), the Divine Mind too has received another, inevitable answer due to 'the huge foreboding mind of Night' (Pg 1, C I: *The Symbol Dawn*, Bk I: *The Book of Beginnings*) that lay 'Across the path of the divine Event', so that it has become 'blind, lost its celestial kingdom of vision, and through that loss its kingdom of glory' (*Author's Note*).

If that is the case it is a sacrifice. When Life sacrificed itself by plunging to the earth, many dawns led eventually to the Mighty Mother's 'first satisfied plan' (Pg 390, C I: *The Destined Meeting-Place,* Bk V: *The Book of Love*) that perhaps preceded the emergence of mind, and where:

"Moved by a universal will of joy
The trees bloomed in their green felicity
And the wild children brooded not on pain."

Now, many dawns later, a second satisfied plan appears in sight in which the Divine Mind will regain vision after the eons-long sacrifice, as affirmed by a boon of Satyavan being born to Dyumatsena. The soul of the world embodying the Knowledge required for Love to be established, means that Divine Mind has to regain vision in the scheme of things, so that Savitri can forever love in the fullness of what Love is. Then too, 'her body's voiceless call' (Pg 9, C I: *The Symbol Dawn, Bk I: The Book of Beginnings*) means something.

In the climb from rung to rung of being, Satyavan, the Supreme's soul, establishes and holds the next status. Occultly that may mean that his soul needs to be present at the dynamic tension between the 'mind of Night' and the 'Divine Mind' to embody something crucial, even as the power of the mind of Night splinters and the power of the Divine Mind grows, so that the next decisive status can be reached. He is also of course present through the entire confrontation between Savitri and Death (Bks VIII, IX, X) and that too surely allows his soul to become acutely discriminative to the dynamics required to change the earth's future.

Satyavan has remained in the area of the destined meeting place since his father's exile. Here there was a deepening in which many siddhis arose. Once Knowledge is established, through the power of Savitri and her conquest of Death, the golden-tower is built, promising a climb unrestrained by the mind of Night.

Then the status of the Supreme's soul that is the soul of the world, can also become the foundation for the flame-child through union with Savitri.

Chapter 9: The Triple Holy Marriage

There is a deep recognition when Savitri and Satyavan meet, and as revealed by the poet, the eternal Lord and Spouse wedded and the united Two began a greater age:

"On the high glowing cupola of the day
Fate tied a knot with morning's halo threads
While by the ministry of an auspice-hour
Heart-bound before the sun, their marriage fire,
The wedding of the eternal Lord and Spouse
Took place again on earth in human forms:
In a new act of the drama of the world
The united Two began a greater age."
(Pg 411, C III: *Satyavan and Savitri,* Bk V: *The Book of Love*)

The Two, the avatar of the Supreme and the eternal universal Mother, the deathless Two-in-One, unite on earth, bringing about an evolutionary leap in the soul of the world. The earth can now become the habitat of the flame-child, allowing aspirations and possibilities without influence from the mind of Night. The perception from on top of the golden-tower is vast and far-reaching. The action is integrated allowing the physical to flower out through material gold.

This start of a greater age is attended by Narad, who has timed his visit to Aswapati's palace just as Savitri returns from her quest. He has materialized on the earthly plane, having journeyed from Paradise, and his cosmic chant ends with the following revelation about the power of love in breaking out of stupors and dreams, into the beyond, and of the lotus-heart of love blooming in the garden of the Spouse:

"He sang to them of the lotus-heart of love
With all its thousand luminous buds of truth,

Which quivering sleeps veiled by apparent things.
It trembles at each touch, it strives to wake
And one day it shall hear a blissful voice
And in the garden of the Spouse shall bloom
When she is seized by her discovered lord.
A mighty shuddering coil of ecstasy
Crept through the deep heart of the universe.
Out of her Matter's stupor, her mind's dreams,
She woke, she looked upon God's unveiled face."
(Pg 418, C I: *The Word of Fate*, Bk VI: *The Book of Fate*)

The lotus-heart of love which strives to wake will bloom in the garden of the Spouse when she is seized by her discovered lord, and the deep heart of the universe will wake and look upon God's unveiled face. This meeting and marriage has cosmic significance, and has taken place again on earth in human forms. Yet, in the canto *The Triple Soul-Forces*, Savitri reveals that the holy marriage is still to be achieved. This requires that Savitri return from her encounter with Death, conquering him, and with luminous Satyavan's hand in hers. She tells the Madonna of Light, a portion of her soul put forth 'To raise the spirit to its forgotten heights', that she must nurse man's hunger for the eternal, fill his yearning heart with heaven's fire, and bring God down into his body and life:

"Madonna of light, Mother of joy and peace,
Thou art a portion of my self put forth
To raise the spirit to its forgotten heights
And wake the soul by touches of the heavens.
Because thou art, the soul draws near to God;
Because thou art, love grows in spite of hate
And knowledge walks unslain in the pit of Night.
But not by showering heaven's golden rain
Upon the intellect's hard and rocky soil
Can the tree of Paradise flower on earthly ground
And the Bird of Paradise sit upon life's boughs
And the winds of Paradise visit mortal air.

Even if thou rain down intuition's rays,
The mind of man will think it earth's own gleam,
His spirit by spiritual ego sink,
Or his soul dream shut in sainthood's brilliant cell
Where only a bright shadow of God can come.
His hunger for the eternal thou must nurse
And fill his yearning heart with heaven's fire
And bring God down into his body and life.
One day I shall return, His hand in mine,
And thou shalt see the face of the Absolute.
Then shall the holy marriage be achieved,
Then shall the divine family be born.
There shall be light and peace in all the worlds."
(Pp 520-1, C IV: *The Triple Soul-Forces*, Bk VII: *The Book of Yoga*)

It seems that for the divine family to be born, man's hunger for the eternal must be nursed, his yearning heart must be filled with heaven's fire, and God must be brought down into his body and life. In other words the flame that animates his soul must become of another nature. The flame must be capable of birthing a flame-child. But this will only happen when the united Two return to earth, and after Savitri has disregarded all temptation offered by the double twilight and the everlasting day, as we shall see in the respective books, Book X: *The Book of the Double Twilight* and Book XI: *The Book of Everlasting Day*. Love too must become of another nature, and this shall be once Knowledge is established with the conquest of Death, Hell, and Night by whose reign knowledge has remained fragmented.

Hence, there is the third holy marriage that must occur. The first and second are implied by the lines (Pg 411) "The wedding of the eternal Lord and Spouse Took place again on earth in human forms", and the third by the lines starting with "One day I shall return, His hand in mine... Then shall the holy marriage be achieved" (Pg 521).

Perhaps the following lines also reveal how such Love is a master ingredient in the flame capable of birthing a flame-child. Delight in oneness sweet and fathomless, embracing of myriad unities seem to be the tones of Love related to the building of the golden tower, and the birth of the flame-child:

"For ever love, O beautiful slave of God!
O lasso of my rapture's widening noose,
Become my cord of universal love.
The spirit ensnared by thee force to delight
Of creation's oneness sweet and fathomless,
Compelled to embrace my myriad unities
And all my endless forms and divine souls.
O Mind, grow full of the eternal peace;
O Word, cry out the immortal litany:
Built is the golden tower, the flame-child born."
(Pg 702, *The Soul's Choice and the Supreme Consummation,* Bk XI: *The Book of Everlasting Day*)

It is for and by the united Two, the deathless Two-in-One, that such a birth that is cased in the safety of the Light must take place. The golden tower and the flame-child also seem to follow the formula of a united two. The golden tower must be related to Satyavan, and the flame-child to Savitri. He becomes the golden tower, a new way in which life is experienced, and a new material grounding that allows the supramental gold to animate and shape matter.

Part of Narad's description in the canto *The Word of Fate* (Pg 430-431) highlights the connection between Satyavan and a tower:

"A will to climb lifts a delight to live,
Heaven's height companion of earth-beauty's charm,
An aspiration to the immortals' air
Lain on the lap of mortal ecstasy.
His sweetness and his joy attract all hearts
To live with his own in a glad tenancy,
His strength is like a tower built to reach heaven,"

Satyavan has also been described by the Supreme in Book XI (Pg 702-3; C I: *The Soul's Choice and the Supreme Consummation*) in the following way:

"He is my soul that climbs from nescient Night
Through life and mind and supernature's Vast
To the supernal light of Timelessness
And my eternity hid in moving Time
And my boundlessness cut by the curve of Space.
It climbs to the greatness it has left behind
And to the beauty and joy from which it fell,
To the closeness and sweetness of all things divine,
To light without bounds and life illimitable,
Taste of the depths of the Ineffable's bliss,
Touch of the immortal and the infinite.
He is my soul that gropes out of the beast
To reach humanity's heights of lucent thought
And the vicinity of Truth's sublime.
He is the godhead growing in human lives
And in the body of earth-being's forms:
He is the soul of man climbing to God
In Nature's surge out of earth's ignorance."

This is not the same Satyavan that existed even as he cried out to her in death 'Savitri, Savitri, O Savitri, Lean down, my soul, and kiss me while I die." (*Death in the Forest*: pg 565). And now luminous Satyavan is the one she shall return with referring to "One day I shall return, His hand in mine". It is with Him that the divine family can be born, because the soul of the world is now ready to also become the flame-child.

Through Her the flame-child is born. She is now embodied Love. More of the unknowable becomes known through her. Even the flame-child can be because of the extraordinary flame in her.

This brings us back to the opening lines of *Savitri* (Pg 1, C I: *The Symbol Dawn*):

"IT WAS the hour before the Gods awake.
Across the path of the divine Event
The huge foreboding mind of Night, alone..."

Because of the journey traced by *Savitri* and the outcome brought about by Savitri, the Gods will awake. But now 'It was the hour before the Gods awake.' 'The divine Event', the supramental manifestation, perhaps is also related to the Gods awaking. These are not gods but Gods, perhaps of the nature that Sri Aurobindo refers to as the 'future mighty Triad' in the *Secret of the Veda* (Pg 491). But now the huge foreboding mind of Night is obstructing the divine Event. But the Gods won't awake here, in matter, unless the voiceless call from Savitri's body is triumphant. For this Satyavan must die. And he has died. And he has come back with Savitri's conquest of Death. But he has come back luminous and ready also, as the soul of the world, to be the cradle in which the flame-child can become. Then the Gods can awake, because now the whole nature of material life has changed.

Chapter 10: The Terrestrial Labor

The terrestrial labor of the earthly avatar of the Supreme and the projections of the eternal, universal Mother has been on-going for eons, as elucidated by the Supreme:

"O Satyavan, O luminous Savitri,
I sent you forth of old beneath the stars,
A dual power of God in an ignorant world,
In a hedged creation shut from limitless self,
Bringing down God to the insentient globe,
Lifting earth-beings to immortality."
(Pg 702, *The Soul's Choice and the Supreme Consummation*, Book XI: *The Book of Everlasting Day*)

Savitri is the Force at work to uplift earth's fate, Satyavan is the Supreme's soul that climbs from nescient Night to the supernal light of Timelessness:

"You are my Force at work to uplift earth's fate,
My self that moves up the immense incline
Between the extremes of the spirit's night and day.
He is my soul that climbs from nescient Night
Through life and mind and supernature's Vast
To the supernal light of Timelessness
And my eternity hid in moving Time
And my boundlessness cut by the curve of Space.
It climbs to the greatness it has left behind
And to the beauty and joy from which it fell,
To the closeness and sweetness of all things divine,
To light without bounds and life illimitable,
Taste of the depths of the Ineffable's bliss,
Touch of the immortal and the infinite."
(Pg 702-3, *The Soul's Choice and the Supreme Consummation*, Book XI: *The Book of Everlasting Day*)

Satyavan is the godhead growing in human lives and in the body of earth-being's forms. Savitri is the Supreme's Power:

"He is my soul that gropes out of the beast
To reach humanity's heights of lucent thought
And the vicinity of Truth's sublime.
He is the godhead growing in human lives
And in the body of earth-being's forms:
He is the soul of man climbing to God
In Nature's surge out of earth's ignorance.
O Savitri, thou art my spirit's Power,
The revealing voice of my immortal Word,
The face of Truth upon the roads of Time
Pointing to the souls of men the routes to God.
(Pg 703, *The Soul's Choice and the Supreme Consummation*, Book XI: *The Book of Everlasting Day*)

The following excerpt from R.Y Deshpande's *Nagin Bhai Tells Me* (Pg 75) gives insight into how the action of terrestrial labor of an Avatar is truly a labor since 'he takes up human action and uses human methods with the human consciousness in front':

"Nagin-bhai: You wrote: "The Avatar is a special manifestation, while for the rest of the time it is the Divine working with the ordinary human limits as a Vibhuti." Does not the Divine find it difficult to mould himself into a Vibhuti and accept the human limits?

Sri Aurobindo: Why should it be difficult? Even the Avatar accepts limits for his work.

Nagin-bhai: Since an Avatar comes here with a divine Power, Light and Ananda why should he pass through the same process of sadhana as an ordinary sadhak?

Sri Aurobindo: The Avatar is not supposed to act in a non-human way—he takes up human action and uses human methods with the human consciousness in front and the Divine behind. If he did not his taking a human body would have no meaning and would be of no use to anybody. He could just as well have stayed above and done things from there."

On 5 May 1954 (CWM, *Words of the Mother – II*), Mother states: "The Divine manifests upon earth whenever and wherever it is possible", and as an illustration, in Volume 3 of the *Agenda* (June 30, 1962), Mother relates how what has been recorded in history is not often how it has actually been. This she knows because incarnations of the Mother have been present through history, and sometimes even four at a time:

"As a child, when I was around ten or twelve years old, I had some rather interesting experiences which I didn't understand at all. I had some history books—you know, the textbooks they give you to learn history. Well, I'd read and suddenly the book would seem to become transparent, or the printed words would become transparent, and I'd see other words or even pictures. I hadn't the faintest idea what was happening to me! And it appeared so natural to me that I thought it was the same for everybody. But my brother and I were great chums (he was only a year and a half older), so I would tell him: "They talk nonsense in history, you know—it is LIKE THIS; it isn't like that: it is LIKE THIS!" And several times the corrections I got on one person or another turned out to be quite exact and detailed. And (I see it now—I understood it later on) they were certainly memories. About some passages I would even say, "How stupid! It was never that; THIS is what was said. It never happened like that; THIS is how it happened." And the book was simply open before me; I was just reading along like any other child and... suddenly something would occur. It was something in me, of course, but I used to think it was in the book!

I found out many, many things about Joan of Arc—many things. And with stunning precision, which made it extremely interesting.

I won't repeat them because I don't remember with exactness, and these things have no value unless they are exact. And then, for the Italian Renaissance: Leonardo da Vinci, Mona Lisa; and for the French Renaissance: François I, Marguerite de Valois, and so forth.

Twice I knew that it wasn't just images but something that had happened to ME, but it took another form. Once (when I was older, around twenty) it happened at Versailles. I had been invited to dinner by a cousin who, with no warning, served me dry champagne during dinner—and I drank it unsuspectingly (I who never drank at all, neither wine nor liquor!).... When I had to get up and cross the crowded room, oh, how very difficult it became, so difficult! Then we went to a place near the chateau, with a view of the whole park. And I was staring at the park, when I saw... I saw the park filling up with lights (the electric lights had vanished), with all kinds of lights, torches, lanterns... and then crowds of people walking about... in Louis XIV dress! I was staring at this with my eyes wide open, holding on to the balustrade to keep from falling down (I wasn't too sure of myself!). I was seeing it all, then I saw myself there, engrossed in conversation with some people (I don't remember now, but there were certain "corrections" here too).... I mean I was a certain person (I don't remember who) and there were those two brothers who were sculptors... anyhow, all kinds of people were there and I saw myself talking, chatting. And I seem to have been sufficiently in control of myself, because when I related all that I had seen, there were some quite interesting details and corrections. That was one time.

There was another time at Blois. They make Anjou wine at Blois. It was the same story: I never drank anything but water or herb tea, but there was a luncheon and they served us sparkling Anjou wine... it seemed so light! Afterwards (I was with an artist friend, we were all artists) we went to see the museum, and it appears I was sparkling with wit! And I suddenly halted in front of a painting by... now let's see, who was it? Coué?... No, Clouet!

Clouet: the princess... one of the princesses. And I started making a few remarks out loud (it took me a little while to notice that people were listening). "Look at this!" I was saying. "Just look at this! Look what this fellow has done to me! See what he's done to me—it wasn't at all like that!" It was actually a beautiful painting, but I was quite unhappy about it: "Look what he's done to me! Look—he made this like that, but that's not at all how it was, it was LIKE THIS!" Details.... And then I became aware (I wasn't too conscious physically)... I realized that people were standing around listening, so I got a grip on myself, and left without a word. But I told my friends, "Listen, it was definitely me! It was MY portrait, it was ME!"

Almost all my memories of past lives came like that; the particular being reincarnated in me rises to the surface and begins acting as if it were all on its own! Once in Italy, when I was fifteen, it happened in an extraordinary way. But that time I did some research. I was in Venice with my mother and I researched in museums and archives, and I discovered my name, and the names of the other people involved. I had relived a scene in the Ducal Palace, but relived it in such a... such an absolutely intense way (laughing—a scene where I was being strangled and thrown into a canal!) that my mother had to hurry me out of there as fast as she could! But that experience I wrote down, so the exact memory has been kept (I didn't write down the other experiences, so the details have all faded away, but this one was noted, although I didn't include any names). The next morning I did some research and uncovered the whole story. I told it all to Théon and Madame Théon, and he also had the memory of a past life there, during the same period. And as a matter of fact, I had seen a portrait there that was the spitting image of Théon! The portrait of one of the doges. It was absolutely (it was a Titian)... absolutely Théon! HIS portrait, you know, as if it had just been done.

All those kinds of things came to me just like that, without my looking for them, wanting them, or understanding them, without doing any sort of discipline, nothing—it was absolutely spontaneous. And they just kept on coming and coming and coming.

From the time I met Théon, it all got clarified: I saw it all clearly, understood and organized it. But a good deal of it happened before—everything I have just told you happened before I met Théon.

(Mother referring to vital beings) One of them was in Murat, on the day of his great victory. It was a vital force that took possession of him and remained just for that victory; and it came into me, so I saw it all! I saw its entry into Murat's body and the whole battle scene—I lived through it all. And once the battle was over, it left him. It was very interesting.

(Mother referring to contemporary incarnations of Mona Lisa and Marguerite de Valois) Yes, but I told you—four at once!

Four at once. And, in general, they were the different states of being of the Mother—the four aspects. Generally one aspect in each embodiment. Or else this or that aspect might have been less present in one embodiment and more present in another. Sometimes there was a fairly central presence and then at the same time less central, less important emanations. But that has happened several times—several times. On two occasions it was particularly clear.

But I have often sensed that there wasn't merely ONE embodiment, that the course of history may have crystallized around this or that person, but there were other embodiments less (how to put it?)... less conspicuous, somewhere else.

They are the different aspects of the Mother."

In *Nagin Bhai Tells Me* (Pp 75-78) there is insight provided by Sri Aurobindo on the multiple lines of the Divine that may simultaneously be acting terrestrially, sometimes as special-purpose Avatars, and constantly as Vibhutis:

"*Nagin-bhai: We believe that both you and the Mother are Avatars. But is it only in this life that both of you have shown your divinity? It is said that you and she have been on the earth constantly since its creation. What were you doing during your previous lives?*

Sri Aurobindo: Carrying on the evolution.

Nagin-bhai: I find it difficult to understand so concise a statement. Can't you elaborate it?

Sri Aurobindo: That would mean writing the whole of human history. I can only say that as there are special descents to carry on the evolution to a farther stage, so also something of the Divine is always there to help through each stage itself in one direction or another.

Nagin-bhai: The common mass of mankind in the past may not have recognized your presence amongst them, especially when outwardly both of you may have had personalities like those of ordinary human beings. But how is it that even Sri Krishna, Buddha or Christ could not detect your presence in this world?

Sri Aurobindo: Presence where and in whom? If they did not meet, they would not recognize, and even if they met there is no reason why the Mother and I should cast off the veil which hung over these personalities and reveal the Divine behind them. Those lives were not meant for any such purpose.

Nagin-bhai: If you were on the earth constantly it would mean that you were here when those great beings descended. Whatever your external cloak, how could you hide your inner self—the true divinity— from them ? It could not have mattered whether you and any of them were born in the same country or not. They ought to have discovered by their own higher light that the Divine Consciousness from which they had descended was already here in a physical form.

Sri Aurobindo: But why can't the inner self be hidden from all in such lives? Your reasoning would only have some force if the presence on earth then were as the Avatar but not if it was only as a Vibhuti.

Nagin-bhai: You have asked, "Presence where and in whom?" Why have you put those question-words? What exactly is conveyed by them?

Sri Aurobindo: ...It is "presence" in or behind some body and behind some outer personality. Also "presence" in what part of the world? If the Mother were in Rome in the time of Buddha, how could Buddha know as he did not even know the existence of Rome?

Nagin-bhai: I did not mean that you or the Mother needed to cast off your veil. It is those Great Men who should have recognized you in spite of the veil.

Sri Aurobindo: One can be a great man without knowing such things as that. Great Men or even great Vibhutis need not be omniscient or know things which it was not useful for them to know.

Nagin-bhai: You said, "But why can't the inner self be hidden from all in such lives?" I fail to understand how anyone could hide one's inner self from Avatars and Vibhutis.

Sri Aurobindo: An Avatar or Vibhuti have the knowledge that is necessary for their work, they need not have more. There was absolutely no reason why Buddha should know what was going on in Rome. An Avatar even does not manifest all the divine omniscience and omnipotence; he has not come for any such unnecessary display; all that is behind him but not in the front of his consciousness. As for the Vibhuti, the Vibhuti need not even know that he is a power of the Divine. Some Vibhutis like Julius Caesar for instance have been atheists. Buddha himself did not believe in a personal God, only in some impersonal and indescribable Permanent.

Nagin-bhai: Still I can't understand one thing; even though you did not cast off your veil, how could people like Buddha or Christ not help casting off their veil (or ignorance) in order to recognise you?

Sri Aurobindo: Why should they? The veil was there necessary for their work. Why should it be thrown off? So if the Mother was present in the life of Christ, she was there not as the Divine Manifestation but as one altogether human. For her to be recognised as the Divine would have created a tremendous disorder and frustrated the work Christ came to do by breaking its proper limits.

Nagin-bhai: You must have heard that just before Christ was born some Rishis from India knew of the divine Descent and set out for Jerusalem merely by their intuition, though they had not known what and where Jerusalem was.

Sri Aurobindo: I never heard of Rishis from India going there. There is a legend of some Magi getting an intuition that a divine Birth was there on earth and following a star that led them to the stable in which Christ was born. But this is a legend, not history.

Nagin-bhai: Since you and the Mother were on earth constantly from the beginning what was the need for Avatars coming down here one after another?

Sri Aurobindo: We were not on earth as Avatars.

68

Nagin-bhai: You say that you both were not on earth as Avatars. And yet you were carrying on the evolution. Since the Divine Himself was on the earth carrying on the evolution, what was the necessity for the coming down of the Avatars who are portions of Himself?

Sri Aurobindo: The Avatar is necessary when a special work is to be done and in crises of the evolution. The Avatar is a special manifestation while for the rest of the time it is the Divine working within the ordinary human limits as a Vibhuti."

Mother also relates the hard labor that was also required to shift specific influences and ways of being in terrestrial becoming (Mother's *Agenda*, Vol 8, 1967, September 6):

"I have made discoveries these last few days.... I have discovered that in past lives (I don't know which ones), my psychic was several times in a tortured body. And it comes back for (how should I put it?) a collective action in the world, on the earth, so that the possibility of the thing may disappear. It's a rather interesting work.

But I noticed it because I said to myself, "But why is my attention constantly turned to that?" Then I looked carefully and saw that the psychic had been in a tortured body several times, long ago at the time of the Inquisition, but also in political cases (much more recently, probably). Real tortures, you know, those inventions in which men are worse than monsters—no animal is more monstrous than human consciousness like that.... And it came back with the "law," the principle of the thing, of the distortion of consciousness, and once I had understood, I looked at myself (I was wondering, "Why? Why is my attention turned to that?"), I then looked and I saw. And I started doing the needful so that it may no longer exist in the creation—some things will not exist any longer.

But nothing in the creation that belongs to the mineral world, the plant world, or the animal world, need disappear. There were those monstrous animals: they disappeared materially, but not ... not the principle of the creation. It's since man came with the mind—when the mind was twisted, deformed by the adverse forces. That is really ugly.

How can that be dissolved? Torture, for instance, that sort of thing? How can it be dissolved from the earth consciousness so it no longer happens again? How can it be done?

Oh, for all really monstrous things, there is only one force—only one force that can dissolve them. I knew it in principle, but now I know it in practice: it is the force of Love. Love is truly all-victorious—but true Love, not what men call "love," not that: true, divine Love.

You see one drop of "That" in its perfection, and all shadows disappear—all disharmony disappears. It can only be in its perfection, in its essential purity.

It truly is all-powerfulness.

And without ... without the sense of victory, that's what is so, so wonderful! It's the All-Victorious which doesn't at all have the sense of being victorious—not at all, at all, at all.

(silence)

This morning for more than an hour, there were veritable scenes (of torture) in their entirety, with all the details, and then ... that wonderful Thing.

Even while the torture is taking place, in that Consciousness it disappears. And it disappears not only for the one who's subjected to it, but for the one who's doing it. And the Thing in itself. It was interesting.

There were all the details of the scene, with such precision! The words uttered, the gestures ... To such an extent that if it had been written simply it would have made an extraordinary novel! That's what surprised me, because I am not a writer, and it doesn't generally interest me, so why did it come back like that, presented so completely?... Until ... until the fulfilment—the end was a marvel: That."

The acceleration in the eons-long terrestrial labor is made clear by the rewriting of a prayer first uttered in 1914 (CWM, Vol 1: Prayers and Meditations, September 25, 1914):

"O divine and adorable Mother, with Thy help what is there that is impossible? The hour of realisations is near and Thou hast assured us of Thy aid that we may perform integrally the supreme Will.

Thou hast accepted us as fit intermediaries between the unthinkable realities and the relativities of the physical world, and Thy constant presence in our midst is a token of Thy active collaboration.

The Lord has willed and Thou dost execute:
A new Light shall break upon the earth.
A new world shall be born,
And the things that were promised shall be fulfilled."

In the April 23, 1956 entry in Mother's *Agenda* (Vol 1) this has been rewritten:

"Lord, Thou hast willed, and I execute:
A new light breaks upon the earth,
A new world is born.
The things that were promised are fulfilled"

Chapter 11: The Double Twilight

Savitri has performed intense yoga and at the culmination of it (Pg 557, C VII: *The Cosmic Spirit and the Cosmic Consciousness*, Bk VII: *The Book of Yoga*) she has realized identity with the cosmic spirit and consciousness:

"Nowhere she dwelt, her spirit was everywhere,
The distant constellations wheeled round her;
Earth saw her born, all worlds were her colonies,
The greater worlds of life and mind were hers;
All Nature reproduced her in its lines,
Its movements were large copies of her own.
She was the single self of all these selves,
She was in them and they were all in her.
This first was an immense identity
In which her own identity was lost:
What seemed herself was an image of the Whole."

She has identified with earth and the soul of the earth:

"She was a subconscient life of tree and flower,
The outbreak of the honied buds of spring;
She burned in the passion and splendour of the rose,
She was the red heart of the passion-flower,
The dream-white of the lotus in its pool.
Out of subconscient life she climbed to mind,
She was thought and the passion of the world's heart,
She was the godhead hid in the heart of man,
She was the climbing of his soul to God.

She has also identified with the cosmos, and than also with Infinity and Eternity:

The cosmos flowered in her, she was its bed.
She was Time and the dreams of God in Time;

She was Space and the wideness of his days.
From this she rose where Time and Space were not;
The superconscient was her native air,
Infinity was her movement's natural space;
Eternity looked out from her on Time."

Further, she has realized the secret of personality:

"An individual, one with cosmic self
In the heart of the Transcendent's miracle
And the secret of World-personality
Was the creator and the lord of all."
(Pg 556, C VII: *The Cosmic Spirit and the Cosmic Consciousness*, Bk VII: *The Book of Yoga*)

This must mean that Death too is seen as a personality in the cosmic mechanism. That's all he is, and nothing more, and her realization means that she is at least equal to that personality and all other personalities that even are cosmic in nature:

Now Savitri is able to proceed into the realms of Death. Now, knowing his thoughts as her own, she is able to debate with him, and knowing him as a temporary albeit necessary movement in the vaster scheme of creation, able also to overcome him.

Identified with the 'mortal' and the 'god and spirit' she was the leader of their march. 'They in front were followers of her will', and being also beyond them she is going to be able to reverse the order of these worlds, even though now that is not the case:

Still was the order of these worlds reversed:
"The mortal led, the god and spirit obeyed
And she behind was leader of their march
And they in front were followers of her will."
(Pg 639, C III: *The Debate of Love and Death*, Bk X: *The Book of the Double Twilight*)

But the reversing of the order suggests two twilights that will occur. Both are necessary for Love to be more fully embodied by Her, and for the golden tower to be built and the flame-child to be born. In other words, for Satyavan, the soul of the world to take an evolutionary leap away from the confines of the mind of Night, and into the foundation where the Gods can awake. First is the shift of Death as he is inundated with Savitri's light, finally being revealed in the figure of the fourfold AUM, as described in the beginning part (Pp 680-3) of *The Book of Everlasting Day*:

"In him the fourfold Being bore its crown
That wears the mystery of a nameless Name,
The universe writing its tremendous sense
In the inexhaustible meaning of a word."
(Pg 680, *The Soul's Choice and the Supreme Consummation*, Bk XI: *The Book of Everlasting Day*)

Second, is the shift of the soul of the earth that will occur as also made evident in *The Book of the Everlasting Day*, with what will shift made clearly evident as if for a last time in *The Dream Twilight of the Earthly Real* (CIV, Bk IX: The Book of the Double Twilight). Here is a one such passage:

"Drifting she saw like pictured fragments flee
Phantoms of human thought and baffled hopes,
The shapes of Nature and the arts of man,
Philosophies and disciplines and laws,
And the dead spirit of old societies,
Constructions of the Titan and the worm.
As if lost remnants of forgotten light,
Before her mind there fled with trailing wings
Dimmed revelations and delivering words,
Emptied of their mission and their strength to save,
The messages of the evangelist gods,
Voices of prophets, scripts of vanishing creeds.
Each in its hour eternal claimed went by:
Ideals, systems, sciences, poems, crafts

Tireless there perished and again recurred,
Sought restlessly by some creative Power;
But all were dreams crossing an empty vast.
...
All things the past has made and slain were there,
Its lost forgotten forms that once had lived,
And all the present loves as new-revealed
And all the hopes the future brings had failed
Already, caught and spent in efforts vain,
Repeated fruitlessly age after age.
Unwearied all returned insisting still
Because of joy in the anguish of pursuit
And joy to labour and to win and lose
And joy to create and keep and joy to kill.
The rolling cycles passed and came again,
Brought the same toils and the same barren end,
Forms ever new and ever old, the long
Appalling revolutions of the world."
(Pp 642-3, C IV: *The Dream Twilight of the Earthly Real*, Bk XI: *The Book of the Double Twilight*)

Chapter 12: Earth's Savitri

When Savitri and Satyavan return to earth all is changed and yet is the same.

But what precisely has changed? To begin with we get hints of how Satyavan and Savitri have undergone change on the very first page of the Canto, *Return to Earth*. 'The weight of heaven' in Satyavan's limbs was felt by the 'waking gladness of her members'. This appears then to be a change at the level of the body, felt also, by her body.

"...The waking gladness of her members felt
The weight of heaven in his limbs, a touch
Summing the whole felicity of things,"
(Pg 715, C I: *Return to Earth*, Bk XII: *Epilogue*)

This is in contrast to Satyavan's earlier body, where the 'violent and hungry hounds of pain' bit his body as they traveled through it:

"But as he worked, his doom upon him came.
The violent and hungry hounds of pain
Travelled through his body biting as they passed..."
(Pg 564, C I: *Death in the Forest*, Bk VIII: *The Book of Death*)

But further, Savitri was now 'earth's Savitri' and there was 'illimitable change' in her: power too great, a bliss too large, a light too intense, love too boundless, as though these things can only be – and in a way that has never been before - because it is in the matter of the earth that it is happening:

"Human she was once more, earth's Savitri,
Yet felt in her illimitable change.
A power dwelt in her soul too great for earth,
A bliss lived in her heart too large for heaven;

Light too intense for thought and love too boundless"
(pg 715, C I: *Return to Earth*, Bk XII: *Epilogue*)

Savitri's earth, the chosen place of her work in the cosmos, has now become such that Savitri has become earth's Savitri. There has been a fundamental change to the soul of the earth, so that it becomes possible for Savitri to be earth's Savitri. The eternal, universal Mother is now also materially of the earth's.

We are reminded also of the raison d'etre for the creation of the world, to experience and to be in love, by these lines:

"The whole wide world clung to her for delight,
Created for her rapt embrace of love."
(Pg 716, C I: *Return to Earth*, Bk XII: *Epilogue*)

In the previous Book and canto (Pg 702, *The Soul's Choice and the Supreme Consummation*, Bk XI: *The Book of the Everlasting Day*) the Supreme had said to Savitri 'For ever love, O beautiful slave of God!', and then again on the very last page of the book (Pg 724) Savitri says the following:

"Awakened to the meaning of my heart
That to feel love and oneness is to live
And this the magic of our golden change,
Is all the truth I know or seek, O sage."

For this active dynamic of love, as we were reminded earlier, Knowledge needs first to exist. With Aswapati's reformatting of Night (Pg 232, Canto VIII: *The World of Falsehood*, Bk II: *The Book of the Traveller of the Worlds*) the basis of fragmentation is changed:

"Torn were the formats of the primal Night
And shattered the stereotypes of Ignorance.
Alive, breathing a deep spiritual breath,
Nature expunged her stiff mechanical code

And the articles of the bound soul's contract,
Falsehood gave back to Truth her tortured shape.
Annulled were the tables of the law of Pain,
And in their place grew luminous characters."

And then in *The Book of the Double Twilight* (Pg 666, Canto IV: *The Dream Twilight of the Earthly Real*) Savitri decisively overcomes Death, signaling the beginning of the end of material fragmentation, and therefore also the beginning of the foundation of Knowledge:

"I hail thee, almighty and victorious Death,
Thou grandiose Darkness of the Infinite.
O Void that makest room for all to be,
Hunger that gnawest at the universe
Consuming the cold remnants of the suns
And eatst the whole world with thy jaws of fire,
Waster of the energy that has made the stars,
Inconscience, carrier of the seeds of thought,
Nescience in which All-Knowledge sleeps entombed
And slowly emerges in its hollow breast
Wearing the mind's mask of bright Ignorance.
Thou art my shadow and my instrument.
I have given thee thy awful shape of dread
And thy sharp sword of terror and grief and pain
To force the soul of man to struggle for light
On the brevity of his half-conscious days.
Thou art his spur to greatness in his works,
The whip to his yearning for eternal bliss,
His poignant need of immortality.
Live, Death, awhile, be still my instrument."

Now on this foundation of Knowledge it is possible for Love to exercise itself, and the utterance of Savitri at the end of the book indicates that huge change where she has awoken to the meaning of her heart so that she, earth's Savitri, will now be able to feel a love 'too boundless'.

Even as she awakes from trance, the earthly reality she experiences has become different. She has fused together space and that in which it arises (Pg 716) being bound by form yet 'Boundless she was, a form of infinity.' She lives in time, yet transcends it, being 'Absorbed no longer by the moment's beat', and the past and future merged in her seamlessly: 'Her spirit the unending future felt And lived with all the unbeginning past.' She was weaving 'old sweet trivial threads', 'into one immortal day', and this whole dynamic of weaving together different realities is echoed again in these lines:

"Ever she held on the paradise of her breast
Her lover charmed into a fathomless sleep,
Lain like an infant spirit unaware
Lulled on the verge of two consenting worlds."
(Pg 716, C I: *Return to Earth*, Bk XII: *Epilogue*)

The soul of the world is becoming the meeting place of two consenting worlds, which also reinforces the earlier line at the beginning of the canto, 'The weight of heaven in his limbs', as is the idea of the golden tower itself, which connects gold, or the supramental, with what is being built.

Earth's Savitri is echoed in the lines by Satyavan when they arise from their positions of trance where the goddess still and pure is made more divine by the sweet human parts that earth has given to Savitri:

"Then filled with the glory of their happiness
They rose and with safe clinging fingers locked
Hung on each other in a silent look.
But he with a new wonder in his heart
And a new flame of worship in his eyes:
"What high change is in thee, O Savitri? Bright
Ever thou wast, a goddess still and pure,
Yet dearer to me by thy sweet human parts

Earth gave thee making thee yet more divine.""
(Pg 718, *The Return to Earth*, BK XII: *Epilogue*)

Satyavan's triple mystic cry, "Savitri, Savitri, O Savitri, Lean down my soul and kiss me while I die", even as he died (Pg 565, *Death in the Forest*, Bk VIII: *The Book of Death*), highlights his complete surrender to her. It is the surrender of mind, life, and body, giving himself entirely to Savitri. Now, with their return to earth, some dynamics of their relationship are made clear by Satyavan in his words to Savitri:

"But now thou seemst almost too high and great
For mortal worship; Time lies below thy feet
And the whole world seems only a part of thee,
Thy presence the hushed heaven I inhabit,
And thou lookst on me in the gaze of the stars,
Yet art the earthly keeper of my soul,
My life a whisper of thy dreaming thoughts,
My morns a gleaming of thy spirit's wings,
And day and night are of thy beauty part."
(Pg 718, *The Return to Earth*, BK XII: *Epilogue*)

Savitri's revealing words highlight the change that has occurred, and how life needs to be lived going forward:

"All now is changed, yet all is still the same.
Lo, we have looked upon the face of God,
Our life has opened with divinity.
We have borne identity with the Supreme
And known his meaning in our mortal lives.
...
Our wedded walk through life begins anew,
No gladness lost, no depth of mortal joy.
Let us go through this new world that is the same,
For it is given back, but it is known,
A playing-ground and dwelling-house of God
Who hides himself in bird and beast and man

Sweetly to find himself again by love,
...
For not for ourselves alone our spirits came
Out of the veil of the Unmanifest,
Out of the deep immense Unknowable
Upon the ignorant breast of dubious earth,
Into the ways of labouring, seeking men,
Two fires that burn towards that parent Sun,
Two rays that travel to the original Light.
To lead man's soul towards truth and God we are born,
To draw the chequered scheme of mortal life
Into some semblance of the Immortal's plan,
To shape it closer to an image of God,
A little nearer to the Idea divine."
(Pg 719-20, *The Return to Earth*, Bk XII: *Epilogue*)

There are other changes that have happened in the previous canto in *The Book of Everlasting Day*. First, is indicated by the name of the canto itself – *The Soul's Choice & The Supreme Consummation*. The *choice* made by Savitri to choose the earth after repeated invitations by the Supreme to enter instead into his Bliss has set into motion all the glorious future and all the realities that Satyavan, the soul of the world, will embody and be the center of in times to come. It is resulting in the Supreme Consummation:

"O beautiful body of the incarnate Word,
Thy thoughts are mine, I have spoken with thy voice.
My will is thine, what thou hast chosen I choose:
All thou hast asked I give to earth and men.
All shall be written out in destiny's book
By my trustee of thought and plan and act,
The executor of my will, eternal Time."
(Pg 698, *The Soul's Choice and Supreme Consummation*, Book XI: *The Book of Everlasting Day*)

In 'The Return to Earth' we see the first clear manifestation of how things are already different when Savitri and Satyavan awake from trance and their journeying into the other realms as covered in Books IX through XI.

We also have the revelation about the golden tower and flame-child (Pg 702, The Soul's Choice and Supreme Consummation, Book XI: The Book of Everlasting Day):

"O Mind, grow full of the eternal peace;
O Word, cry out the immortal litany:
Built is the golden tower, the flame-child born."

And then we have the phenomenon of Savitri and Satyavan being accompanied by Krishna and Kali as they return to earth:

"Pursuing her in her fall, implacably sweet,
A face was over her which seemed a youth's,
Symbol of all the beauty eyes see not,
Crowned as with peacock plumes of gorgeous hue
Framing a sapphire, whose heart-disturbing smile
Insatiably attracted to delight,
Voluptuous to the embraces of her soul.
Changed in its shape, yet rapturously the same,
It grew a woman's dark and beautiful
Like a mooned night with drifting star-gemmed clouds,
A shadowy glory and a stormy depth,
Turbulent in will and terrible in love."
(Pg 711, The Souls Choice and the Supreme Consummation, Book XI The Book of Everlasting Day)

The Mother comments on Sri Aurobindo's aphorisms (477, 478, 479) to do with Krishna and Kali (CWM, Vol 10: *On Thoughts and Aphorisms, Fourth Period of Commentaries* (1969-70)), where their presence indicates that the world will change into the model of heaven:

"477—When will the world change into the model of heaven? When all mankind becomes boys and girls together with God revealed as Krishna and Kali, the happiest boy and strongest girl of the crowd, playing together in the gardens of Paradise. The Semitic Eden was well enough, but Adam and Eve were too grown up and its God Himself too old and stern and solemn for the offer of the Serpent to be resisted.

478—The Semites have afflicted mankind with the conception of a God who is a stern and dignified king and solemn judge and knows not mirth. But we who have seen Krishna, know Him for a boy fond of play and a child full of mischief and happy laughter.

479—A God who cannot smile could not have created this humorous universe.

Ridicule is the strongest weapon against the powers of falsehood. With a single sentence, Sri Aurobindo annihilates the power of one of these man-made gods."

While we have seen some of the changes to Satyavan and Savitri earlier in this canto, now we will see some other changes to the world itself.

There is a significant change to King Dyumatsena. This must mean then that the Divine Mind is no longer blind, that it has regained its kingdom of vision and glory. So the earth that Savitri and Satyavan have returned to, is now different even by this change:

"In front King Dyumatsena walked, no more
Blind, faltering-limbed, but his far-questing eyes
Restored to all their confidence in light
Took seeingly this imaged outer world;
Firmly he trod with monarch step the soil.
By him that queen and mother's anxious face".
(Pg 722, *The Return to Earth*, Book XII: *Epilogue*)

Then there is the deepening redder gold in Savitri's physical body itself:

'Then all eyes turned their wondering looks where stood,
A deepening redder gold upon her cheeks,
With lowered lids the noble lovely child,
And one consenting thought moved every breast.
"What gleaming marvel of the earth or skies
Stands silently by human Satyavan
To mark a brilliance in the dusk of eve?
If this is she of whom the world has heard,
Wonder no more at any happy change.
Each easy miracle of felicity
Of her transmuting heart the alchemy is."
(Pg 723, *The Return to Earth*, Book XII: *Epilogue*)

About red and gold, in an experience about the supramental ship Mother relates (CWM, Vol. 9: *Q&A 1957-1958*, 19 February 1958): "This substance was of the most material supramental, the supramental substance which is closest to the physical world, the first to manifest. The light was a mixture of gold and red, forming a uniform substance of a luminous orange."

To a query by a priest and sage about the light and power revealed with her, she answers, revealing the embodied Love:

"Awakened to the meaning of my heart
That to feel love and oneness is to live
And this the magic of our golden change,
Is all the truth I know or seek, O sage."
Wondering at her and her too luminous words
Westward they turned in the fast-gathering night.'
(Pg 724, The Return to Earth, Book XII: Epilogue)

Finally is the reality of Savitri nursing in her bosom a greater dawn:

'Then while they skirted yet the southward verge,
Lost in the halo of her musing brows
Night, splendid with the moon dreaming in heaven
In silver peace, possessed her luminous reign.
She brooded through her stillness on a thought
Deep-guarded by her mystic folds of light,
And in her bosom nursed a greater dawn.'
(Pg 724, *The Return to Earth*, Book XII: *Epilogue*)

The change becomes abundantly apparent when we contrast it with the scene of the morn earlier in that very same day, in the first canto, *The Symbol Dawn,* where the world is also described as the 'green smiling dangerous world'. Savitri's life shares the cosmic load with its 'yoke of ignorance and fate', and 'the labour and stress of mortal days':

"But now she stirred, her life shared the cosmic load.
At the summons of her body's voiceless call
Her strong far-winging spirit travelled back,
Back to the yoke of ignorance and fate,
Back to the labour and stress of mortal days,
Lighting a pathway through strange symbol dreams
Across the ebbing of the seas of sleep.
Her house of Nature felt an unseen sway,
Illumined swiftly were life's darkened rooms,
And memory's casements opened on the hours
And the tired feet of thought approached her doors."
(Pg 9, C I: *The Symbol Dawn*, Bk I: *The Book of Beginnings*)

This world was one in which ancient disputants from time immemorial – Earth and Love and Doom – wrestled in the Night, and in the shadow of her heart at the very center of the debate was one who 'saw grief's timeless depths but not life's goal':

"All came back to her: Earth and Love and Doom,
The ancient disputants, encircled her

Like giant figures wrestling in the night:
The godheads from the dim Inconscient born
Awoke to struggle and the pang divine,
And in the shadow of her flaming heart,
At the sombre centre of the dire debate,
A guardian of the unconsoled abyss
Inheriting the long agony of the globe,
A stone-still figure of high and godlike Pain
Stared into Space with fixed regardless eyes
That saw grief's timeless depths but not life's goal."
(Pg 9-10, C I: *The Symbol Dawn*, Bk I: *The Book of Beginnings*)

And amidst this reality Savitri of the 'green smiling dangerous world' (Pg 10) Savitri arose to confront Time and Fate, forever changing all the future.

Chapter 13: Savitri's Dawn

The very last line of the epic ends with the following:

"She brooded through her stillness on a thought
Deep-guarded by her mystic folds of light,
And in her bosom nursed a greater dawn."
(Pg 724, *The Return to Earth*, Book XII: *Epilogue*)

Savitri nurses in her bosom a greater dawn. And this dawn surely has to do with 'her body's voiceless call'. The last line of Canto 1, *The Symbol Dawn*, is 'This was the day when Satyavan must die.' The earthly body of the soul of the world must die, only to return more luminous in deep union with Savitri, his other self, so that even the body can be fulfilled going forward.

Thus far life on earth is brief. A mere moment in which a struggling soul at best works out some infinitesimal piece in an infinite plot. The mind of Night has assured that, with its formidable allies of Death, Hell, the Sons of Darkness, the Mother of Evil, and the World of Falsehood.

But all that is now changing due to the action of the triple avatars. Many dawns have led to this time, where the Universal Mother comes in her fullness as Savitri. For eons she projected only parts of her self to help earth in its preparation. But now the decisive time has come, and the 'greater dawn' that Savitri nurses in her bosom is unlike any other that has preceded it.

While the second half of *The Symbol Dawn*, when 'Savitri too awoke among these tribes' clearly lays out the burden of man, the age-old strife between formidable godheads, and the lines that lead to a greater dawn, even in the esoteric first half of the *The Symbol Dawn* we already have hints that this greater dawn the Savitri's Dawn, is different.

To begin with, the Earth, the special planet whose soul is the soul of the Supreme, opposes even in its 'formless stupor' the 'vain enormous trance of Space':

"Athwart the vain enormous trance of Space,
Its formless stupor without mind or life,
A shadow spinning through a soulless Void,
Thrown back once more into unthinking dreams,
Earth wheeled abandoned in the hollow gulfs
Forgetful of her spirit and her fate."
(Page 1, C I: *The Symbol Dawn*, Bk I: *The Book of Beginnings*)

There is something in the Earth that appears not to have forgotten, and further is the place where a swift awakening takes place, with a 'persistent thrill' resulting in 'beauty and wonder' disturbing 'the fields of God', and the revelation and the flame poured out:

"The darkness failed and slipped like a falling cloak
From the reclining body of a god.
Then through the pallid rift that seemed at first
Hardly enough for a trickle from the suns,
Outpoured the revelation and the flame."
(Page 3, C I: *The Symbol Dawn*, Bk I: *The Book of Beginnings*)

A tremendous Dawn is prepared, and buried in the hours:

"Dawn built her aura of magnificent hues
And buried its seed of grandeur in the hours."

This Dawn houses a significant myth and signs of it are penned with sky for page:

"Interpreting a recondite beauty and bliss
In colour's hieroglyphs of mystic sense,
It wrote the lines of a significant myth
Telling of a greatness of spiritual dawns,

A brilliant code penned with the sky for page."
(Page 4, C I: *The Symbol Dawn*, Bk I: *The Book of Beginnings*)

As the Mother says, the significant myth is the story of Savitri, and in the following lines we see that the omniscient Goddess, 'the eternal universal Mother, Mother of all universes from all eternity' (*Mother's Agenda*), is getting ready to incarnate on earth, where she and the soul of the earth, Satyavan, will do their work that changes everything forever:

"A Form from far beatitudes seemed to near.
Ambassadress twixt eternity and change,
The omniscient Goddess leaned across the breadths
That wrap the fated journeyings of the stars
And saw the spaces ready for her feet."
(Page 4, C I: *The Symbol Dawn*, Bk I: *The Book of Beginnings*)

And the omniscient Goddess looks behind for 'her veiled sun':

"Once she half looked behind for her veiled sun,
Then, thoughtful, went to her immortal work."
(Page 4, C I: *The Symbol Dawn*, Bk I: *The Book of Beginnings*)

Is this the same sun of whom Savitri is the daughter ("Savitri is the Divine Word,
daughter of the Sun, goddess of the supreme Truth who comes down and is born to save" – *Author's Note*)?

In the Vedas there is a hymn to Savitri, the Sun-God, with Sri Aurobindo's explanatory note:

"The Rishi hymns the Sun-God as the source of divine knowledge and the creator of the inner worlds. To him, the Seer, the seekers of light yoke their mind and thoughts; he, the one knower of all forms of knowledge, is the one supreme ordainer of the sacrifice. He assumes all forms as the robes of his being and his creative sight and creates the supreme good and happiness for the two

forms of life in the worlds. He manifests the heavenly world, shining in the path of the dawn of divine knowledge; in that path the other godheads follow him and it is his greatness of light that they make the goal of all their energies. He has measured out for us our earthly worlds by his power and greatness: but it is in the three worlds of light that he attains to his real greatness of manifestation in the rays of the divine sun; then he encompasses the night of our darkness with his being and his light and becomes Mitra who by his laws produces the luminous harmony of our higher and lower worlds. Of all our creation he is the one author, and by his forward marches he is its increaser until the whole world of our becoming grows full of his illumination."
(*Hymn to Savitri, Secret of the Veda*)

This action of Savitri, the Sun-God, to "encompasses the night of our darkness with his being and his light and becomes Mitra who by his laws produces the luminous harmony of our higher and lower worlds" "until the whole world of our becoming grows full of his illumination" must hint at the greater dawn she nurses in her bosom. But the beginning point of this action of the Sun-God is where Sri Aurobindo's epic appears to end, with Savitri and Satyavan returning to earth, and in Mother's *Agenda* (January 22, 1961) she states, referring to Sri Aurobindo's writing of *Savitri*:

"He says that she very carefully takes the SOUL of Satyavan into her arms, like a little child, to pass through all the realms and come back down to earth.

He hasn't forgotten a single detail to make it easy to understand—for someone who knows how to understand. And it is when Savitri reaches the earth that Satyavan regains his full human stature."

So at the end of the epic Satyavan regains his full human stature. What does this mean though? The full human stature perhaps refers to the fact that the 'golden tower' has now been built, or since it is a litany, is being built ("O Word, cry out the immortal litany: Built is the golden tower, the flame-child born.", Pg 702). But *Savitri* was completed in 1950. We may assume then that in Mother's on-going work, the golden tower has been built.

But what did that take? That took the work of the triple avatars.

First Aswapati had to break through human and cosmic bounds, and roam freely in his larger Self. He traversed the world on the World-Stair, changed the dynamics of constraining worlds to break down future opposition, and created a new world in his inner realms, before he finally received a boon from the Divine Mother that she would incarnate as Savitri.

Then Satyavan had to hold in himself the burden and opposition between the mind of Night and the fallen Divine Mind, had to attain Siddhis in the Mighty Mother's forest which lay as per her first satisfied plan, and completely surrender to Savitri in life and in death.

Savitri, even as a child, began to change the world by her influence. And as she grew, she made all the world her own, and found her other self. She performed yoga to break free from the grip of ego, to discover her parts of herself that have helped and guided the world and promise them their path to fulfilment, to break free from cosmos, enter into Nothingness, house all potentiality, become equal and even greater than any cosmic personality, even Death, become the great Divine Mother, the creative force from which everything past, present, and future arises, and just as she marginalizes temptation from Death, she simply marginalizes temptation even from the Supreme.

When she returns to earth, the result is Satyavan in his full human stature, the golden tower, that can now also see freely and far, become the flame-child, and be the ground on which all future dawns shall be established.

The epic *Savitri* itself appears to be only the very beginning of the *Savitri's Dawn* hinted at in the first half of *The Symbol Dawn*. We have to turn to other parts of *Savitri* to get a sense for what the Savitri's dawn may mean.

Chapter 14: Fourfold Dawns

The full human stature, the golden tower, is a prerequisite to future dawns. Savitri nursed a greater dawn in her bosom. It was the fruit of the work of three avatars, and is the foundation for further dawns. In *The Book of the Divine Mother* (Book III) we get a hint of what some of this may look like when Aswapati dialogues with the Divine Mother. There is a prophesy foreseeing the architects of immortality (*The Vision & The Boon*: pp 342-5). Aswapati speaks of 'a larger seeing man with nobler heart', one that surely exists only after Satyavan has reached his full human-stature:

"In anguish we labour that from us may rise
A larger-seeing man with nobler heart,
A golden vessel of the incarnate Truth,
The executor of the divine attempt
Equipped to wear the earthly body of God,
Communicant and prophet and lover and king."
(Pg 342, C IV: *The Vision and the Boon*, Bk III: *The Book of the Divine Mother*)

And interestingly it appears that in that last line 'Communicant and prophet and lover and king' there is more of the direct action of the four Solar Kings and the Mother's four powers, with a possible primary mapping with 'communicant' perhaps correlating with Mahasaraswati, 'prophet' with Maheshwari, 'lover' with Mahalakshmi, and 'king' with Mahakali. But these powers can only exist fully in the full human stature. Prior to that there is too much of a mixture dictated by the hold of the mind of Night and its formidable allies. Now it means that more of the four powers of the Mother are flowing through human beings. There is greater union between the human and the Divine Mother.

Aswapati refers to the 'strange irrational product of the mire':

"This strange irrational product of the mire,
This compromise between the beast and god,
Is not the crown of thy miraculous world."
(Pg 343, C IV: *The Vision and the Boon*, Bk III: *The Book of the Divine Mother*)

But this 'strange irrational product of the mire' is becoming a thing of the past even as the Divine Mind becomes operative instead of the mind of Night:

"Overpassed were the leaden formulas of the Mind,
Overpowered the obstacle of mortal Space:
The unfolding Image showed the things to come."
(Pg 343, C IV: *The Vision and the Boon*, Bk III: *The Book of the Divine Mother*)

In *Secret of the Veda*, Sri Aurobindo refers to the 'future might Triad': "…Vishnu, Rudra, Brahmanaspati, the future mighty Triad, preside over the indispensable conditions". About Rudra he says: "…the other in his wrath and might and violent beneficence forces onward the great evolution and smites the opponent and the recusant and the ill-doer".
(pg 491, *Secret of the Veda*).

And this sheds light on the 'giant dance of Shiva' in the ongoing vision:

"A giant dance of Shiva tore the past;
There was a thunder as of worlds that fall;
Earth was o'errun with fire and the roar of Death
Clamouring to slay a world his hunger had made;
There was a clangour of Destruction's wings:
The Titan's battle-cry was in my ears,
Alarm and rumour shook the armoured Night."
(Pg 343, C IV: *The Vision and the Boon*, Bk III: *The Book of the Divine Mother*)

Aswapati sees the 'Omnipotent's flaming pioneers' who crossed 'the twilight of an age' and here again we see the clear action of the four powers of The Mother. Maheshwari mapping to 'The sun-eyed children of a marvellous dawn, The great creators with wide brows of calm'; Mahakali with 'The massive barrier-breakers of the world And wrestlers with destiny in her lists of will'; Mahasaraswati to 'The labourers in the quarries of the gods, The messengers of the Incommunicable, The architects of immortality'; and Mahalakshmi to 'Faces that wore the Immortal's glory still, Voices that communed still with the thoughts of God, Bodies made beautiful by the spirit's light, Carrying the magic word, the mystic fire, Carrying the Dionysian cup of joy, Approaching eyes of a diviner man, Lips chanting an unknown anthem of the soul', implying again that these powers can act only once the soul of the world, Satyavan, has now embodied the full human stature:

"I saw the Omnipotent's flaming pioneers
Over the heavenly verge which turns towards life
Come crowding down the amber stairs of birth;
Forerunners of a divine multitude,
Out of the paths of the morning star they came
Into the little room of mortal life.
I saw them cross the twilight of an age,
The sun-eyed children of a marvellous dawn,
The great creators with wide brows of calm,
The massive barrier-breakers of the world
And wrestlers with destiny in her lists of will,
The labourers in the quarries of the gods,
The messengers of the Incommunicable,
The architects of immortality.
Into the fallen human sphere they came,
Faces that wore the Immortal's glory still,
Voices that communed still with the thoughts of God,
Bodies made beautiful by the spirit's light,
Carrying the magic word, the mystic fire,

Carrying the Dionysian cup of joy,
Approaching eyes of a diviner man,
Lips chanting an unknown anthem of the soul,
Feet echoing in the corridors of Time."
(Pg 343-4, C IV: *The Vision and the Boon*, Bk III: *The Book of the Divine Mother*)

He further relates the outcome of the 'crowding down the amber stairs of birth' by the 'Forerunners of the divine multitude' resulting in the change to the 'suffering earth'. The change in the soul that has already taken place thereby firmly holding a different possibility in place gets expressed by the external change that justifies 'the light on Nature's face':

"High priests of wisdom, sweetness, might and bliss,
Discoverers of beauty's sunlit ways
And swimmers of Love's laughing fiery floods
And dancers within rapture's golden doors,
Their tread one day shall change the suffering earth
And justify the light on Nature's face."
(Pg 344, C IV: *The Vision and the Boon*, Bk III: *The Book of the Divine Mother*)

This Fourfold Dawn appears imminent, if not already on-going, and points too, to the greater dawns that require that the fourfold powers of the Mother be grounded and active as suggested in Sri Aurobindo's, The Mother – "Only when the Four have founded their harmony and freedom of movement in the transformed mind and life and body, can those other rarer Powers manifest in the earth movement and the supramental action become possible" (SABCL, *Vol 25: The Mother*, VI):

"There are other great Personalities of the Divine Mother, but they were more difficult to bring down and have not stood out in front with so much prominence in the evolution of the earth-spirit. There are among them Presences indispensable for the supramental realisation,—most of all one who is her Personality of that mysterious and powerful ecstasy and Ananda which flows from a supreme divine Love, the Ananda that alone can heal the gulf between the highest heights of the supramental spirit and the lowest abysses of Matter, the Ananda that holds the key of a wonderful divinest Life and even now supports from its secrecies the work of all the other Powers of the universe. But human nature bounded, egoistic and obscure is inapt to receive these great Presences or to support their mighty action. Only when the Four have founded their harmony and freedom of movement in the transformed mind and life and body, can those other rarer Powers manifest in the earth movement and the supramental action become possible. For when her Personalities are all gathered in her and manifested and their separate working has been turned into a harmonious unity and they rise in her to their supramental godheads, then is the Mother revealed as the supramental Mahashakti and brings pouring down her luminous transcendences from their ineffable ether. Then can human nature change into dynamic divine nature because all the elemental lines of the supramental Truth-consciousness and Truth-force are strung together and the harp of life is fitted for the rhythms of the Eternal."

Chapter 15: Awakening the Superman

In the realm of everlasting day (*The Book of Everlasting Day*) the Supreme puts Savitri's and Satyavan's eons long journey in context also giving insight into the ways in which it will continue to change.

He describes the current condition where knowledge is trapped, life is hauled by desire, and Matter hides the soul:

"In the world of my knowledge and my ignorance
Where God is unseen and only is heard a Name
And knowledge is trapped in the boundaries of mind
And life is hauled in the drag-net of desire
And Matter hides the soul from its own sight..."
(Pg 702, *The Soul's Choice and the Supreme Consummation*, Book XI: *The Book of Everlasting Day*)

He then begins to describe how things will change through the travails of the dual incarnate power of God – Satyavan and Savitri. There are many stages, initiated by the awareness of God:

"Yet shall they look up as to peaks of God
And feel God like a circumambient air
And rest on God as on a motionless base.
Yet shall there glow on mind like a horned moon
The Spirit's crescent splendour in pale skies
And light man's life upon his Godward road."
(Pg 703-4, *The Soul's Choice and the Supreme Consummation*, Book XI: *The Book of Everlasting Day*)

While now 'mind is all and its uncertain ray', it is still 'the thought-driven chariot of the soul' that will lead 'to vistas of a far uncertain dawn' and to the threshold of 'greater destinies mind cannot surmise':

"But more there is concealed in God's Beyond
That shall one day reveal its hidden face.
Now mind is all and its uncertain ray,
Mind is the leader of the body and life,
Mind the thought-driven chariot of the soul
Carrying the luminous wanderer in the night
To vistas of a far uncertain dawn,
To the end of the Spirit's fathomless desire,
To its dream of absolute truth and utter bliss.
There are greater destinies mind cannot surmise"
(Pg 704, *The Soul's Choice and the Supreme Consummation*, Book XI: *The Book of Everlasting Day*)

He prophesies that 'The Spirit's mightiness shall cast off its mask' and 'It's greatness shall be felt shaping the world's course':

"Mind is not all his tireless climb can reach,
There is a fire on the apex of the worlds,
There is a house of the Eternal's light,
There is an infinite truth, an absolute power.
The Spirit's mightiness shall cast off its mask;
Its greatness shall be felt shaping the world's course:
It shall be seen in its own veilless beams,
A star rising from the Inconscient's night,
A sun climbing to Supernature's peak."
(Pg 704, *The Soul's Choice and the Supreme Consummation*, Book XI: *The Book of Everlasting Day*)

What has been stabilized by Satyavan by achieving the full human stature through union with Savitri, also allowing the Divine Mind to increasingly operate without the influence of the mind of Night, will allow more humans to abandon the 'dubious middle Way'. Some of these will feel in Savitri 'the secret Force' and become 'Adventurers into a Mightier Day' to step 'into the Truth, the Right, the Vast':

"Abandoning the dubious middle Way,

A few shall glimpse the miraculous Origin
And some shall feel in you the secret Force
And they shall turn to meet a nameless tread,
Adventurers into a mightier Day.
Ascending out of the limiting breadths of mind,
They shall discover the world's huge design
And step into the Truth, the Right, the Vast.
You shall reveal to them the hidden eternities,
The breath of infinitudes not yet revealed,
Some rapture of the bliss that made the world,
Some rush of the force of God's omnipotence,
Some beam of the omniscient Mystery."
(Pg 704, *The Soul's Choice and the Supreme Consummation*, Book XI: *The Book of Everlasting Day*)

Even, 'when the hour of the Divine draws near' the Mighty Mother shall herself take birth and 'the Truth supreme be given to men' (Pg 705). These shall yet be in forms made ready by the lives of Satyavan and Savitri, and will be in human clay. The question then is, has this already taken place in the birth of the lives of Sri Aurobindo and The Mother? Sri Aurobindo wrote 'The Hour of God' between 1914 – 1919. This would imply that it already is, and therefore that the Mighty Mother has already taken birth in Time. The fact that the Mighty Mother has already taken birth is also made clear by the Mother in her *Agenda* (Vol. 3, June 30, 1962):

"None of those beings, those gods and deities of various pantheons, have the same rapport with the Supreme that man has; for man has a psychic being, in other words, the Supreme's presence within him. These gods are emanations—independent emanations—created for a special purpose and a particular action which they fulfill SPONTANEOUSLY; they do it not with a sense of constant surrender to the Divine but simply because that's what they are, and why they are, and all they know is what they are. They don't have the conscious link with the Supreme that man has—man carries the Supreme within himself.

That makes a considerable difference.

But with this present incarnation of the Mahashakti…. She is the Supreme's first manifestation, creation's first stride, and it was She who first gave form to all those beings. Now, since her incarnation in the physical world, and through the position She has taken here in relation to the Supreme by incarnating in a human body, all the other worlds have been influenced, and influenced in an extremely interesting way. I have been in contact with all those gods, all those great beings, and for the most part their attitude has changed. And even with those who didn't want to change, it has nonetheless influenced their way of being."

Further, reference to 'God be born into the human clay' in CWM (Vol 20, Oct 11 1943) The Mother says:

"There is one Divine embodied upon the earth. He is Sri Aurobindo and his Word is for the manifestation."

Sri Aurobindo has already stated that he will incarnate in the first supramental body built in the supramental way. That never stopped him though from being 'born into the human clay' in the meanwhile.

So the following lines suggest that this has already happened:

"But when the hour of the Divine draws near
The Mighty Mother shall take birth in Time
And God be born into the human clay
In forms made ready by your human lives.
Then shall the Truth supreme be given to men:
There is a being beyond the being of mind,
An Immeasurable cast into many forms,
A miracle of the multitudinous One,
There is a consciousness mind cannot touch,
Its speech cannot utter nor its thought reveal.

It has no home on earth, no centre in man,
Yet is the source of all things thought and done,
The fount of the creation and its works,
It is the origin of all truth here,
The sun-orb of mind's fragmentary rays,
Infinity's heaven that spills the rain of God,
The Immense that calls to man to expand the Spirit,
The wide Aim that justifies his narrow attempts,
A channel for the little he tastes of bliss."
(Pg 705, *The Soul's Choice and the Supreme Consummation*, Book XI: *The Book of Everlasting Day*)

In the *Hour of God* (CWSA Vol 12, *Essays Human and Divine* [1914 – 1919], Pg 147) there is already a very different modus operandi that is being required of humans, with little effort producing great results and changing destinies. Foundational to this is purity, and discrimination as it relates to the dictates of earthly prudence:

"There are moments when the Spirit moves among men and the breath of the Lord is abroad upon the waters of our being; there are others when it retires and men are left to act in the strength or the weakness of their own egoism. The first are periods when even a little effort produces great results and changes destiny; the second are spaces of time when much labour goes to the making of a little result. It is true that the latter may prepare the former, may be the little smoke of sacrifice going up to heaven which calls down the rain of God's bounty. Unhappy is the man or the nation which, when the divine moment arrives, is found sleeping or unprepared to use it, because the lamp has not been kept trimmed for the welcome and the ears are sealed to the call. But thrice woe to them who are strong and ready, yet waste the force or misuse the moment; for them is irreparable loss or a great destruction.

In the hour of God cleanse thy soul of all self-deceit and hypocrisy and vain self-flattering that thou mayst look straight into thy spirit and hear that which summons it. All insincerity of nature, once thy defence against the eye of the Master and the light of the ideal, becomes now a gap in thy armour and invites the blow. Even if thou conquer for the moment, it is the worse for thee, for the blow shall come afterwards and cast thee down in the midst of thy triumph. But being pure cast aside all fear; for the hour is often terrible, a fire and a whirlwind and a tempest, a treading of the winepress of the wrath of God; but he who can stand up in it on the truth of his purpose is he who shall stand; even though he fall, he shall rise again, even though he seem to pass on the wings of the wind, he shall return. Nor let worldly prudence whisper too closely in thy ear; for it is the hour of the unexpected, the incalculable, the immeasurable. Mete not the power of the Breath by thy petty instruments, but trust and go forward.

But most keep thy soul clear, even if for a while, of the clamour of the ego. Then shall a fire march before thee in the night and the storm be thy helper and thy flag shall wave on the highest height of the greatness that was to be conquered."

To the degree that we are able to follow the way laid out in the *Hour of God*, the following lines related also to Aswapati's vision about the 'Omnipotent's flaming pioneers' in the 'The Vision and the Boon' will perhaps become truer:

"Some shall be made the glory's receptacles
And vehicles of the Eternal's luminous power.
These are the high forerunners, the heads of Time,
The great deliverers of earth-bound mind,
The high transfigurers of human clay,
The first-born of a new supernal race."
(Pg 705, *The Soul's Choice and the Supreme Consummation*, Book XI: *The Book of Everlasting Day*)

This further, shall lead to the waking of the superman in mortal man:

"The incarnate dual Power shall open God's door,

Eternal supermind touch earthly Time.
The superman shall wake in mortal man
And manifest the hidden demigod
Or grow into the God-Light and God-Force
Revealing the secret deity in the cave."
(Pg 705, *The Soul's Choice and the Supreme Consummation*, Book XI: *The Book of Everlasting Day*)

These words from Sri Aurobindo (Pp. 150-52, CWSA Vol 12, *Essays Human and Divine, The Divine Superman*) shed insight into how the superman is to be created, and further, its relations with gods:

"This is thy work and the aim of thy being and that for which thou art here, to become the divine superman and a perfect vessel of the Godhead. All else that thou hast to do, is only a making thyself ready or a joy by the way or a fall from thy purpose. But the goal is this and the purpose is this and not in power of the way and the joy by the way but in the joy of the goal is the greatness and the delight of thy being. The joy of the way is because that which is drawing thee is also with thee on thy path and the power to climb was given thee that thou mightest mount to thy own summits.

If thou hast a duty, this is thy duty; if thou ask what shall be thy aim, let this be thy aim; if thou demand pleasure, there is no greater joy, for all other joy is broken or limited, the joy of a dream or the joy of a sleep or the joy of self-forgetting. But this is the joy of thy whole being. For if thou say what is my being, this is thy being, the Divine, and all else is only its broken or its perverse appearance. If thou seek the Truth, this is the Truth. Place it before thee and in all things be faithful to it.

It has been well said by one who saw but through a veil and mistook the veil for the face, that thy aim is to become thyself; and he said well again that the nature of man is to transcend himself. This is indeed his nature and that is indeed the divine aim of his self-transcending.

What then is the self that thou hast to transcend and what is the self that thou hast to become? For it is here that thou shouldst make no error; for this error, not to know thyself, is the fountain of all thy grief and the cause of all thy stumbling.

That which thou hast to transcend is the self that thou appearest to be, and that is man as thou knowest him, the apparent Purusha. And what is this man? He is a mental being enslaved to life and matter; and where he is not enslaved to life and matter, he is the slave of his mind. But this is a great and heavy servitude; for to be the slave of mind is to be the slave of the false, the limited and the apparent. The self that thou hast to become, is the self that thou art within behind the veil of mind and life and matter. It is to be the spiritual, the divine, the superman, the real Purusha. For that which is above the mental being, is the superman. It is to be the master of thy mind, thy life and thy body; it is to be a king over Nature of whom thou art now the tool, lifted above her who now has thee under her feet. It is to be free and not a slave, to be one and not divided, to be immortal and not obscured by death, to be full of light and not darkened, to be full of bliss and not the sport of grief and suffering, to be uplifted into power and not cast down into weakness. It is to live in the Infinite and possess the finite. It is to live in God and be one with him in his being. To become thyself is to be this and all that flows from it.

Be free in thyself, and therefore free in thy mind, free in thy life and thy body. For the Spirit is freedom.

Be one with God and all beings; live in thyself and not in thy little ego. For the Spirit is unity.

Be thyself, immortal, and put not thy faith in death; for death is not of thyself, but of thy body. For the Spirit is immortality.

To be immortal is to be infinite in being and consciousness and bliss; for the Spirit is infinite and that which is finite lives only by his infinity.

These things thou art, therefore thou canst become all this; but if thou wert not these things, then thou couldst never become them. What is within thee, that alone can be revealed in thy being. Thou appearest indeed to be other than this, but wherefore shouldst thou enslave thyself to appearances?

Rather arise, transcend thyself, become thyself. Thou art man and the whole nature of man is to become more than himself. He was the man-animal, he has become more than the animal man. He is the thinker, the craftsman, the seeker after beauty. He shall be more than the thinker, he shall be the seer of knowledge; he shall be more than the craftsman, he shall be the creator and master of his creation; he shall be more than the seeker of beauty, for he shall enjoy all beauty and all delight. Physical, he seeks for his immortal substance; vital he seeks after immortal life and the infinite power of his being; mental and partial in knowledge, he seeks after the whole light and the utter vision.

To possess these is to become the superman; for [it] is to rise out of mind into the supermind. Call it the divine mind or Knowledge or the supermind; it is the power and light of the divine will and the divine consciousness. By the supermind the Spirit saw and created himself in the worlds, by that he lives in them and governs them. By that he is Swarat Samrat, self-ruler and all-ruler.

Supermind is superman; therefore to rise beyond mind is the condition.

To be the superman is to live the divine life, to be a god; for the gods are the powers of God. Be a power of God in humanity.

To live in the divine Being and let the consciousness and bliss, the will and knowledge of the Spirit possess thee and play with thee and through thee, this is the meaning.

This is the transfiguration of thyself on the mountain. It is to discover God in thyself and reveal him to thyself in all things. Live in his being, shine with his light, act with his power, rejoice with his bliss. Be that Fire and that Sun and that Ocean. Be that joy and that greatness and that beauty.

When thou hast done this even in part, thou hast attained to the first steps of supermanhood."

In the Mother's *Agenda* entry of January 8, 1969 (Vol 10, Pg 26) The Mother speaks of the descent of the superman consciousness:

"It was on the 1st of January after midnight. I woke up at 2 in the morning, surrounded by a consciousness, but so concrete, and NEW, in the sense that I had never experienced that. It lasted, quite concrete and present, for two or three hours, and then it spread out and went to find all those who could receive it. And at the same time I knew it was the consciousness of the superman, that is, the intermediary between man and the supramental being.

It has given the body a sort of assurance, a sort of trust. That experience has made it steady, as it were, and if it keeps the true attitude, all the support is there to help it.

A certain number of people (I asked afterwards) had the experience, they felt it (not as clearly), felt the presence of a new consciousness—lots of people. They told me (I asked them if they had felt something), they told me, "Oh, yes!" But each with... (Mother twists her fingers slightly) naturally his own special approach."

It is clear then that the superman is already amongst us. The only question is, how wide is the awakening? How many have already become the superman?

Chapter 16: Immortality and Magic Order

For the Supreme to touch the earth the superman has to have woken in mortal man. Else the Supreme's touch shall mean little:

"Then shall the earth be touched by the Supreme"
(Pg 705, *The Soul's Choice and the Supreme Consummation*, Book XI: *The Book of Everlasting Day*)

The touch of the Supreme will have a host of effects including the annulment of death and pain. The formulas of the Ignorance will be erased, and the being will become ready for immortality:

"His bright unveiled Transcendence shall illumine
The mind and heart and force the life and act
To interpret his inexpressible mystery
In a heavenly alphabet of Divinity's signs.
His living cosmic spirit shall enring,
Annulling the decree of death and pain,
Erasing the formulas of the Ignorance,
With the deep meaning of beauty and life's hid sense,
The being ready for immortality,
His regard crossing infinity's mystic waves
Bring back to Nature her early joy to live,
The metred heart-beats of a lost delight,
The cry of a forgotten ecstasy,
The dance of the first world-creating Bliss."
(Pg 705-6, *The Soul's Choice and the Supreme Consummation*, Book XI: *The Book of Everlasting Day*)

Earth-nature shall be ruled by eternity's law:

"The Immanent shall be the witness God
Watching on his many-petalled lotus-throne
His actionless being and his silent might
Ruling earth-nature by eternity's law,

A thinker waking the Inconscient's world,
An immobile centre of many infinitudes
In his thousand-pillared temple by Time's sea."
(Pg 706, *The Soul's Choice and the Supreme Consummation*, Book XI: *The Book of Everlasting Day*)

The embodied being will be 'a point or line drawn in the Infinite', and 'the Eternal's truth shall be his light and guide'. This means that the immortality of the being, though not yet of the body, has become real:

"Then shall the embodied being live as one
Who is a thought, a will of the Divine,
A mask or robe of his divinity,
An instrument and partner of his Force,
A point or line drawn in the infinite,
A manifest of the Imperishable.
The supermind shall be his nature's fount,
The Eternal's truth shall mould his thoughts and acts,
The Eternal's truth shall be his light and guide."
(Pg 706, *The Soul's Choice and the Supreme Consummation*, Book XI: *The Book of Everlasting Day*)

With the immortality of the being a different operative order has to also have become real. This is perhaps a 'magic order' which will overtop the mechanical universe and lead to 'a mightier race' inhabiting 'the mortal's world'. Then there will be men and supermen, the latter reigning as the king of life, leading man towards God:

"All then shall change, a magic order come
Overtopping this mechanical universe.
A mightier race shall inhabit the mortal's world.
On Nature's luminous tops, on the Spirit's ground,
The superman shall reign as king of life,
Make earth almost the mate and peer of heaven,
And lead towards God and truth man's ignorant heart

And lift towards godhead his mortality."
(Pg 706, *The Soul's Choice and the Supreme Consummation*, Book XI: *The Book of Everlasting Day*)

But physical immortality must be something else as suggested by the process in which first the psychic being gets integrated with its instruments so that there is a single consciousness, and second when the supramental consciousness can hold 'these births as if strung on one single thread'. (CWM, Vol 3, Q&A 1930 – 1931, Pg 149):

"For, as a rule, the physical mind and the physical vital dissolve with the death of the organism: they disintegrate and return to the universal Nature and nothing remains of their experiences. Not until they have become united with the psychic, so that there are not two halves but a single consciousness, the whole nature unified round the central Divine Will and this centralised being is connected up with the divine line of consciousness which is above—not until this happens can one receive the knowledge belonging to that consciousness and become aware of the entire series of forms and lives which were upheld by it as its own successive means of gradual self-expression. Before this is done, it is meaningless to speak of one's past births and their various incidents. This precious oneself is just the present impermanent exterior nature which has absolutely nothing to do with the several other formations behind which, as behind the present one, the true being stands. Only the supramental consciousness holds these births as if strung on one single thread and that alone can give the real knowledge of them all."

And further:

"A power released from circumscribing bounds,
Its height pushed up beyond death's hungry reach,
Life's tops shall flame with the Immortal's thoughts,
Light shall invade the darkness of its base."

(Pg 706-7, *The Soul's Choice and the Supreme Consummation*, Book XI: *The Book of Everlasting Day*)

These lines describing a power pushing up 'beyond death's hungry reach' and 'Light shall invade the darkness of' Life's base', seem also to be a consequence of the being becoming immortal, and further, may be a bridge to a 'conscious entity' at the level of the cells described by a passage in the *Agenda* (*Agenda*, Vol 13, April 26, 1972, pp 167-9). This may be because immortality in being perhaps heightens the sense of 'ridiculousness' of time-bound human consciousness and requires 'indifference'. Mother describes how the consciousness in the cells must aggregate and form into a 'conscious entity' capable of being conscious of Matter as well as conscious of the Supramental:

"Oh, it's so interesting. So interesting. Since childhood, I have always endeavored, as it were, to attain total indifference—nothing is annoying, nothing is pleasant. Since childhood, I recall a consciousness striving for... for indifference. Interesting! It makes me understand why he said that it was I who could attempt the transition between human consciousness and supramental consciousness. He said that. He said it to me and he says it here (it's written among Nirod's things). Now I understand why....

...What's more, it feels awful and ridiculous. Ridiculous and awful. It's the first effect of the consciousness of what has to be, it exerts a pressure. Even higher humanity is an awful and ridiculous thing for the overmind (Mother corrects herself), for the supramental ("supramental" is a word I don't like too much; I understand why Sri Aurobindo used it, he didn't want "superman"—it's not superman at all). There is a far greater difference between a supramental being and a human being than between a human being and a chimpanzee.

But the difference is not so much external: it's a difference of consciousness. I can sense it, I sense it so vividly, and so close! When I am very still, it comes, from over there, and even the highest and most intellectual human consciousness is ridiculous in comparison.

...It does permeate, but.... To be exact, we can say that it permeates with difficulty, but it does permeate. That's what causes the impression that life is awful. Personally, I feel that life is downright ridiculous—grotesque. Grotesque.

(silence)

One must be thoroughly convinced of it before one can expect to receive that Consciousness. You know what I would say? It's a good sign—it's not pleasant, but it's a good sign.

But, of course, at best—at the very best—we are transitional beings. And well, transitional beings.... But the consciousness of the inner being ultimately gets stronger, you follow? Stronger even than the consciousness of the material being. So the material being can be dissolved, but the inner consciousness remains stronger. It is of that consciousness that we can say, 'This is me.'

There you are. THAT is the important thing.

As for me, the purpose of this body is now simply: the Command and the Will of the Lord, so I can do as much groundwork as possible. But it isn't the Goal at all. You see, we don't know, we don't have the slightest knowledge of what the supramental life is. Therefore we don't know if this (Mother pinches the skin of her hand) can change enough to adapt or not—and to tell the truth, I am not worried about it, it's not a problem that preoccupies me too much; the problem I am preoccupied with is building that supramental consciousness So IT becomes the being. It's that consciousness which must become the being. That's what's important. As for the rest, we'll see (it's the same as worrying over a change of clothing). But it must truly be IT, you see. And in order to do that, all the consciousness contained in these cells must aggregate, form and organize itself into an independent conscious entity—the consciousness in the cells must aggregate and form into a conscious entity capable of being conscious of Matter as well as conscious of the Supramental. That's the thing. That's what is being done. How far will we be able to go? I don't know."

And perhaps the body remembering God (following lines in *Savitri*) follows from the 'conscious entity' described by the Mother.

"Then in the process of evolving Time
All shall be drawn into a single plan,
A divine harmony shall be earth's law,
Beauty and joy remould her way to live:
Even the body shall remember God,
Nature shall draw back from mortality
And Spirit's fires shall guide the earth's blind force;
Knowledge shall bring into the aspirant Thought
A high proximity to Truth and God."
(Pg 706-7, *The Soul's Choice and the Supreme Consummation*, Book XI: *The Book of Everlasting Day*)

But this also implies that immortality as mentioned previously ('The being ready for immortality', Pg 706) is different from physical immortality. The body remembering God seems to be a prerequisite for physical immortality.

In the *Agenda* (Vol 8, January 21, 1967) the Mother relates how during transition at the physical level there must be a faith in the sole real existence of the Supreme:

"Something still rather indefinable is happening.

The body was in the habit of fulfilling its functions automatically, as something natural, which means that for it, the question of their importance or usefulness did not arise: it didn't have that mental vision, for instance, or vital vision of things, of what's "important" or "interesting" and what isn't. That didn't exist. But now that the cells are becoming conscious, they seem to step back (Mother makes a gesture of stepping back): they look at themselves, they begin to watch themselves act, and they very much wonder, "What's the use of all this?" And then, an aspiration: "How? How should things truly be? What's our function, our usefulness, our basis? Yes, what should be our basis and our 'standard' of life?" To express it mentally again, we could say, "How will we be when we are divine? What will be the difference? What's the divine way of being?" And there, what speaks is that whole kind of physical base which is entirely made up of thousands of small things absolutely indifferent in themselves, whose raison d'être is only as a whole, as a totality, like a support to another action, but which in themselves seem devoid of any meaning. And then, it's again the same thing: a sort of receptivity, of silent opening to let oneself be permeated, and a very subtle perception of a way of being that would be luminous, harmonious.

That way of being is still quite indefinable; but in this search there is a constant perception (which translates itself in vision) of a multicoloured light, of all the colours—all the colours not in layers but as though (stippling gesture) a combination of dots, of all the colours. Two years ago (a little more than two years, I don't remember), when I met the Tantrics, when I came into contact with them, I started seeing that light, and I thought it was the "tantric light," the tantric way of seeing the material world. But now, I see it constantly, associated with everything, and it seems to be what we might call a "perception of true Matter." All possible colours are combined without being mixed together (same stippling gesture), and combined in luminous dots. Everything is as though made up of this. And it seems to be the true mode of being—I am not yet sure, but in any case it's a far more conscious mode of being.

I see it all the time: with eyes open, eyes closed, all the time. And one has a strange perception (for the body), a strange perception of subtlety, permeability (if I may call it that), of suppleness of form, and not exactly an elimination but a considerable lessening of the rigidity of forms (the rigidity is eliminated, but not the forms: a suppleness in the forms). And for the body itself, the first few times it felt that in some part or the other, it had the impression of … being a bit lost, with the sense of something eluding it. But if one remains very quiet and waits quietly, it's simply replaced by a sort of plasticity and fluidity that seems to be a new mode of the cells.

It would be probably what on the material level must take the place of the physical ego; that is to say, the rigidity of the form seems to have to give way to this new way of being. Of course, the first contact is always very … surprising. But the body is getting used to it little by little. What's a little difficult is the moment of transition from one way to the other. It's done very progressively, yet at the moment of transition there are a few seconds that are … the least we can say is "unexpected."

In that way, all habits are undone. It's the same with all the functionings: blood circulation, digestion, breathing—all the functions. And at the moment of transition, it's not that one abruptly takes the place of the other, but there is a state of fluidity between the two which is … difficult. It's only because of that great Faith, a perfectly still, luminous, constant, immutable faith in the real existence of the supreme Lord—in the SOLE real existence of the Supreme—that everything goes on apparently as it is.

There are as if great waves of all the ordinary movements, ordinary ways of being, ordinary habits, which are pushed back and which come back again, and try to engulf and are pushed back again. And I can see that for years the body and the whole body consciousness used to rush back into the old way to seek safety, as a measure of safety, in order to elude; but now, the body has been persuaded not to do it any more and on the contrary to accept, "Well, if it's dissolution, let it be dissolution." But it accepts what will be.

Mentally, when that happens in the physical mind (it was years ago, but I had observed that), it's what gives people the feeling that they're going insane, and they get frightened (and with fear things happen), so they rush back into ordinary common sense to escape it. It's the equivalent—not the same thing, but the equivalent of what happens in the material: you feel all the usual stability is vanishing. Well, for a long time—a long time—there was that retreat into habit, and then you are quite at peace and you start all over again. But now, the cells no longer want that "Come what may, we'll see!" The great adventure.

How will we be?—How will we be? How ... You understand, it's the cells asking, "How should we be? How will we be?"

It's interesting."

Chapter 17: The Supramental World

Therefore to become immortal in the sense of there being conscious remembrance and even perhaps linking from life to life to advance the line of consciousness that a string of lives is part of, requires realization of the supramental consciousness.

Then the supermind will claim the world for light and the Immortal's fire kindle earthly hearts:

"The supermind shall claim the world for Light
And thrill with love of God the enamoured heart
And place Light's crown on Nature's lifted head
And found Light's reign on her unshaking base.
A greater truth than earth's shall roof-in earth
And shed its sunlight on the roads of mind;
A power infallible shall lead the thought,
A seeing Puissance govern life and act,
In earthly hearts kindle the Immortal's fire."
(Pg 707, *The Soul's Choice and the Supreme Consummation*, Book XI: *The Book of Everlasting Day*)

In regard to the preceding lines the Mother shares in the *Agenda* the fact that the supramental world already exists, that she is permanently there in a supramental body, and that what needs to be done is that an intermediate zone between the physical world and the supramental world needs to be built. She describes the experience of a huge ship where this is being done.

(Agenda, Vol 1, February 3, 1958, pp 137-43):
"Between the beings of the supramental world and men, there exists approximately the same gap as between men and animals. Sometime ago, I had the experience of identification with animal life, and it is a fact that animals do not understand us; their consciousness is so constituted that we elude them almost

entirely. And yet I have known domestic animals—cats and dogs, but especially cats—who made an almost yogic effort of consciousness to understand us. But generally, when they watch us living and acting, they don't understand, they don't SEE US as we are and they suffer because of us. We are a constant enigma to them Only a very tiny part of their consciousness is linked to us. And it is the same for us when we try to look at the supramental world. Only when the link of consciousness has been built shall we see it—and even then, only that part of our being which has undergone the transformation will be capable of seeing it as it is—otherwise the two worlds would remain as separate as the animal world and the human world.

The experience I had on February 3 proves this. Before, I had had an individual, subjective contact with the supramental world, whereas on February 3, I went strolling there in a concrete way—as concretely as I used to go strolling in Paris in times past—in a world that EXISTS IN ITSELF, beyond all subjectivity.

It is like a bridge being built between the two worlds.

This is the experience as I dictated it immediately thereafter:

(silence)

The supramental world exists in a permanent way, and I am there permanently in a supramental body. I had proof of this today when my earthly consciousness went there and consciously remained there between two and three o'clock in the afternoon: I now know that for the two worlds to join in a constant and conscious relationship what is missing is an intermediate zone between the existing physical world and the supramental world as it exists. This zone has yet to be built, both in the individual consciousness and in the objective world, and it is being built. When formerly I used to speak of the new world that is being created, I was speaking of this intermediate zone. And similarly, when I am on 'this' side—that is, in the realm of the physical consciousness—and I see the supramental power, the supramental light and substance constantly permeating matter, I am seeing and participating in the construction of this zone.

I found myself upon an immense ship, which is the symbolic representation of the place where this work is being carried out. This ship, as big as a city, is thoroughly organized, and it had certainly already been functioning for quite some time, for its organization was fully developed. It is the place where people destined for the supramental life are being trained. These people (or at least a part of their being) had already undergone a supramental transformation because the ship itself and all that was aboard was neither material nor subtle-physical, neither vital nor mental: it was a supramental substance. This substance itself was of the most material supramental, the supramental substance nearest the physical world, the first to manifest. The light was a blend of red and gold, forming a uniform substance of luminous orange. Everything was like that—the light was like that, the people were like that—everything had this color, in varying shades, however, which enabled things to be distinguished from one another. The overall impression was of a shadowless world: there were shades, but no shadows. The atmosphere was full of joy, calm, order; everything worked smoothly and silently. At the same time, I could see all the details of the education, the training in all domains by which the people on board were being prepared.

This immense ship had just arrived at the shore of the supramental world, and a first batch of people destined to become the future inhabitants of the supramental world were about to disembark. Everything was arranged for this first landing. A certain number of very tall beings were posted on the wharf. They were not human beings and never before had they been men. Nor were they permanent inhabitants of the supramental world. They had been delegated from above and posted there to control and supervise the landing. I was in charge of all this since the beginning and throughout. I myself had prepared all the groups. I was standing on the bridge of the ship, calling the groups forward one by one and having them disembark on the shore. The tall beings posted there seemed to be reviewing those who were disembarking, allowing those who were ready to go ashore and sending back those who were not and who had to continue their training aboard the ship. While standing there watching everyone, that part of my consciousness coming from here became extremely interested: it wanted to see, to identify all the people, to see how they had changed and to find out who had been taken immediately as well as those who had to remain and continue their training. After awhile, as I was observing, I began to feel pulled backwards and that my body was being awakened by a consciousness or a person from here1—and in my consciousness, I protested: 'No, no, not yet! Not yet! I want to see who's there!' I was watching all this and noting it with intense interest … It went on like that until, suddenly, the clock here began striking three, which violently jerked me back. There was the sensation of a sudden fall into my body. I came back with a shock, but since I had been called back very suddenly, all my memory was still intact. I remained quiet and still until I could bring back the whole experience and preserve it.

The nature of objects on this ship was not that which we know upon earth; for example, the clothes were not made of cloth, and this thing that resembled cloth was not manufactured—it was a part of the body, made of the same substance that took on different forms. It had a kind of plasticity. When a change had to be made, it was done not by artificial and outer means but by an inner working, by a working of the consciousness that gave the substance its form or appearance. Life created its own forms. There was ONE SINGLE substance in all things; it changed the nature of its vibration according to the needs or uses.

Those who were sent back for more training were not of a uniform color; their bodies seemed to have patches of a grayish opacity, a substance resembling the earth substance. They were dull, as though they had not been wholly permeated by the light or wholly transformed. They were not like this all over, but in places.

The tall beings on the shore were not of the same color, at least they did not have this orange tint; they were paler, more transparent. Except for a part of their bodies, only the outline of their forms could be seen. They were very tall, they did not seem to have a skeletal structure, and they could take on any form according to their needs. Only from their waists to their feet did they have a permanent density, which was not felt in the rest of their body. Their color was much more pallid and contained very little red, it verged rather on gold or even white. The parts of whitish light were translucid; they were not absolutely transparent, but less dense, more subtle than the orange substance.

Just as I was called back, when I was saying, 'Not yet … ,' I had a quick glimpse of myself, of my form in the supramental world. I was a mixture of what these tall beings were and the beings aboard the ship. The top part of myself, especially my head, was a mere silhouette of a whitish color with an orange fringe. The more it approached the feet, the more the color resembled that of the people on the ship, or in other words, orange; the more it went up towards the top, the more translucid and white it was, and the red faded. The head was only a silhouette with a brilliant sun at its center; from it issued rays of light which were the action of the will.

As for the people I saw aboard ship, I recognized them all. Some were here in the Ashram, some came from elsewhere, but I knew them as well. I saw everyone, but as I realized that I would not remember everyone when I came back, I decided not to give any names. Besides, it is unnecessary. Three or four faces were very clearly visible, and when I saw them, I understood the feeling that I have had here, on earth, while looking into their eyes: there was such an extraordinary joy … On the whole, the people were young; there were very few children, and their ages were around fourteen or fifteen, but certainly not below ten or twelve (I did not stay long enough to see all the details). There were no very old people, with the exception of a few. Most of the people who had gone ashore were of a middle age—again, except for a few. Several times before this experience, certain individual cases had already been examined at a place where people capable of being supramentalized are examined; I had then had a few surprises which I had noted—I even told some people. But those whom I disembarked today I saw very distinctly. They were of a middle age, neither young children nor elderly people, with only a few rare exceptions, and this quite corresponded to what I expected. I decided not to say anything, not to give any names. As I did not stay until the end, it would be impossible for me to draw an exact picture, for it was neither absolutely clear nor complete. I do not want to say things to some and not say them to others.

What I can say is that the criterion or the judgment was based EXCLUSIVELY on the substance constituting the people—whether they belonged completely to the supramental world or not, whether they were made of this very special substance. The criterion adopted was neither moral nor psychological. It is likely that their bodily substance was the result of an inner law or an inner movement which, at that time, was not in question. At least it is quite clear that the values are different.

When I came back, along with the memory of the experience, I knew that the supramental world was permanent, that my presence there is permanent, and that only a missing link is needed to allow the consciousness and the substance to connect—and it is this link that is being built. At that time, my impression (an impression which remained rather long, almost the whole day) was of an extreme relativity—no, not exactly that, but an impression that the relationship between this world and the other completely changes the criterion by which things are to be evaluated or judged. This criterion had nothing mental about it, and it gave the strange inner feeling that so many things we consider good or bad are not really so. It was very clear that everything depended upon the capacity of things and upon their ability to express the supramental world or be in relationship with it. It was so completely different, at times even so opposite to our ordinary way of looking at things! I recall one little thing that we usually consider bad ... actually how funny it was to see that it is something excellent! And other things that we consider important were really quite unimportant there! Whether it was like this or like that made no difference. What is very obvious is that our appreciation of what is divine or not divine is incorrect. I even laughed at certain things ... Our usual feeling about what is anti-divine seems artificial, based upon something untrue, unliving (besides, what we call life here appeared lifeless in comparison with that world); in any event, this feeling should be based upon our relationship between the two worlds and according to whether things make this relationship easier or more difficult. This would thus completely change our evaluation of what brings us nearer to the Divine or what takes us away from Him. With people, too, I saw that what helps them or prevents them from becoming supramental is very different from what our ordinary moral notions imagine. I felt just how ... ridiculous we are.

(Then Mother speaks to the children)

There is a continuation to all this, which is like the result in my consciousness of the experience of February 3, but it seems premature to read it now. It will appear in the April issue [of the Bulletin], as a sequel to this.

But one thing—and I wish to stress this point to you—which now seems to me to be the most essential difference between our world and the supramental world (and it is only after having gone there consciously, with the consciousness that ordinarily works here, that this difference appeared to me in what might be called its enormity): everything here, except for what happens within and at a very deep level, seemed absolutely artificial to me. Not one of the values of ordinary physical life is based upon truth. Just as we have to buy cloth, sew it together, then put it on our backs in order to dress ourselves, likewise we have to take things from outside and then put them inside our bodies in order to feed ourselves. For everything, our life is artificial.

A true, sincere, spontaneous life, as in the supramental world, is a springing forth of things through the fact of conscious will, a power over substance that shapes this substance according to what we decide it should be. And he who has this power and this knowledge can obtain whatever he wants, whereas he who does not has no artificial means of getting what he desires.

In ordinary life, EVERYTHING is artificial. Depending upon the chance of your birth or circumstances, you have a more or less high position or a more or less comfortable life, not because it is the spontaneous, natural and sincere expression of your way of being and of your inner need, but because the fortuity of life's circumstances has placed you in contact with these things. An absolutely worthless man may be in a very high position, and a man who might have marvelous capacities of creation and organization may find himself toiling in a quite limited and inferior position, whereas he would be a wholly useful individual if the world were sincere.

It is this artificiality, this insincerity, this complete lack of truth that appeared so shocking to me that ... one wonders how, in a world as false as this one, we can arrive at any truthful evaluation of things.

But instead of feeling grieved, morose, rebellious, discontent, I had rather the feeling of what I spoke of at the end: of such a ridiculous absurdity that for several days I was seized with an uncontrollable laughter whenever I saw things and people! Such a tremendous laughter, so absolutely inexplicable (except to me), because of the ridiculousness of these situations.

When I invited you on a voyage into the unknown, a voyage of adventure, I did not know just how true were my words! And I can promise those who are ready to embark upon this adventure that they will make some very astonishing discoveries."

When Sri Aurobindo left his physical body, Mother relates:

"When I asked Him (December 8, 1950) to resuscitate his body, He clearly answered: "I have left this body purposely. I will not take it back. I shall manifest again in the first supramental body built in the supramental way."
(The Mother, CWM, Vol 13, Pg 9)

She also comments about the uncertainty of the timing of when this may happen that could even be 500 years from now"

"One can't fix the precise time of His return.

It may even be five hundred years later. I can't say anything, since the knowledge has not come to me.

I only say things when I get them."

In *Savitri*, description of future dawns continues, where even man, let alone the superman, 'shall forget consent to mortality', and ' an ignorant evolution's hierarchy release the Wisdom chained below its base':

"The Spirit's eyes shall look through Nature's eyes,
The Spirit's force shall occupy Nature's force.
This world shall be God's visible garden-house,
The earth shall be a field and camp of God,
Man shall forget consent to mortality
And his embodied frail impermanence.
This universe shall unseal its occult sense,
Creation's process change its antique front,
An ignorant evolution's hierarchy

Release the Wisdom chained below its base."
(Pg 707-8, *The Soul's Choice and the Supreme Consummation,*
Book XI: *The Book of Everlasting Day*)

Chapter 18: Psychic Being's Materialization

Reference the announcement, 'Built is the golden tower, the flame-child born', the golden tower is that which has arisen with the progressive unfoldment of of the soul of the world, His incarnation as it has lived, aspired, and moved from rung to rung of being, changing its forms and all its dynamics along the way. Now it has become a golden tower, one in which it is to be assumed, supramentalization becomes possible. It is a tower, an unfolding that has been disenfranchised from the mind of Night, and being the soul of the world, of this earth that Savitri has chosen to do her work on, becomes the foundation for all future unfoldment. The supramental being, yes: but even before that the progressive foundation for all intermediate beings between the human and the supramental.

And the flame-child has now also been born. In Book IV, *The Book of Birth and Quest*, there are two cantos, C I: *The Birth and Childhood of the Flame*, and C II: *The Growth of the Flame*. These already refer to Savitri. And yet after that she has done intense yoga, as recounted in Book VII: *The Book of Yoga*, and further, has overcome all manner of temptation offered by Death and the Supreme himself, not to mention conquering Death as recounted on Pg 666 in Book X: *The Book of the Double Twilight*, in C IV: *The Dream Twilight of the Earthly Real*.

There is also a hint as to the nature of that flame in the flame-child in *The Book of Yoga* (Pg 501, C III: *The Entry into the Inner Countries*) when Savitri is about to embark on 'the great winding road' that leads to her soul, that has been pointed to by one in a company of luminous gods:

"And Savitri mingling in that glorious crowd,
Yearning to the spiritual light they bore,
Longed once to hasten like them to save God's world;
But she reined back the high passion in her heart;

She knew that first she must discover her soul."

There must be the discovery of the soul. Then it is the conscious psychic being completely aligned with the Divine Mother that is at at the forefront. The flame then also would be of a different nature than if aspiration and surrender were being conducted by an individual not in realization of their soul.

In *Letters on Yoga* (CWSA, *Letters on Yoga-III, The Fundamental Realizations of the Integral Yoga*), Sri Aurobindo states:

"The psychic fire is the fire of aspiration, purification and tapasya which comes from the psychic being. It is not the psychic being, but a power of the psychic being.

The psychic being is a Purusha, not a flame—the psychic fire is not the being, it is something proper to it.

That the constant fire of aspiration has to be lit is true; but this fire is the psychic fire and it is lit or burns up and increases as the psychic grows within and for the psychic to grow quietude is needful.

Such an attitude encourages the opening of the psychic and would therefore bring at once the psychic joy and the kindling of Agni in the psychic centre."

So it could be the case that due to what Savitri has done in terms of her yoga and work, her psychic fire becomes the crucible for the emergence of the flame-child. This must then refer to a new principle, one also with no links to the mind of Night, or to any influences from Hell or the Sons of Darkness. This may also relate to the new creation that Aswapati initiated in the inner worlds, just before his audience with the Divine Mother, where a new knowledge, that needed not a sheath of Ignorance, became a cosmos' seed:

"A Bliss, a Light, a Power, a flame-white Love
Caught all into a sole immense embrace;
Existence found its truth on Oneness' breast
And each became the self and space of all.
The great world-rhythms were heart-beats of one Soul,
To feel was a flame-discovery of God,
All mind was a single harp of many strings,
All life a song of many meeting lives;
For worlds were many, but the Self was one.
This knowledge now was made a cosmos' seed:
This seed was cased in the safety of the Light,
It needed not a sheath of Ignorance."
(Pp 323-3, C III: *The House of the Spirit and the New Creation*, Bk III: *The Book of the Divine Mother*)

The golden tower being built, which given that Satyavan is the soul of the earth, means that the connection between matter and golden possibilities is now real, and further, that because of that the flame-child can also become a reality for inhabitants of the earth. This is so because Satyavan is Savitri's other and second self.

A short message from the Mother on June 24, 1972 states: "It is indispensable that each one finds his psychic and unites with it definitively. It is through the psychic that the supramental will manifest itself."

Is the flame-child, then, the same thing as the supramental being? If the flame-child is born from a particular kind of psychic fire, one that has become from the kind of tapasya and love as shown by Savitri, than perhaps this is the case.

Referring to the psychic being, Sri Aurobindo writes (*CWSA, Letters on Yoga-1, The Parts of the Being and the Planes of Consciousness*):

"It grows in the consciousness by Godward experience, gaining strength every time there is a higher movement in us, and, finally, by the accumulation of these deeper and higher movements there is developed a psychic individuality,—that which we call usually the psychic being. It is always this psychic being that is the real, though often the secret cause of man's turning to the spiritual life and his greatest help in it.

The psychic is a spark come from the Divine which is there in all things and as the individual evolves it grows in him and manifests as the psychic being, the soul seeking always for the Divine and the Truth and answering to the Divine and the Truth whenever and wherever it meets it.

There is always a part of the mind, of the vital, of the body which is or can be influenced by the psychic; they can be called the psychic-mental, the psychic-vital, the psychic-physical. According to the personality or the degree of evolution of each person, this part can be small or large, weak or strong, covered up and inactive or prominent and in action.

Become aware of that and put all your mental, vital and physical nature in relation to it, in order that they may become purified, harmonised, divinised, and the supramental being and nature may descend and be manifested in you—for until this is done, this conscious linking and relation with the psychic centre, there can be no supramental descent."

The Mother relates her experience of the psychic being becoming the supramental being (*Agenda*, Vol 11, 1970, July 1, pp 244-6):

"I had an experience which I found interesting, because it was the first time. It was yesterday or the day before (I forget), R. was here, just in front of me, kneeling, and I saw her psychic being towering above by this much (gesture about eight inches), taller. It's the first time. Her physical being was short, and the psychic being was tall, like this. And it was a sexless being: neither man nor woman. So I said to myself (it may be always that way, I don't know, but at that time I noticed it very clearly), I said to myself, "But the psychic being is the one that will materialize and become the supramental being!"

I saw it, it was like that. There were distinctive features, but not very pronounced, and it was clearly a being that was neither male nor female, that had features of both combined. And it was taller than her, it exceeded her on every side by about this much (gesture extending beyond the physical being by about eight inches). She was here, and it was like this (gesture). Its color was… this color that, if it became very material, would be Auroville's color [orange]. It was softer, as if behind a veil, it wasn't absolutely precise, but it was this color. And there was hair, but… it was something else.

Another time maybe I'll see better.

But I found it very interesting, because that being seemed to tell me, "You're wondering what the supramental being will be—here it is! Here it is, this is it." And it was there. It was her psychic being.

Then one understands. One understands: the psychic being will materialize… and it gives a continuity to evolution.

This creation gives you a clear impression that nothing is arbitrary, that there is a sort of divine logic behind, which isn't like our human logic, but highly superior to our logic (but it exists), and that logic was fully satisfied when I saw that.

It's odd, it was also when R. was here that I had that experience of the supramental light going through within [Mother] without causing any shadow. R. has something like that, I don't know…. And this time, it's really interesting. I was quite interested. It was there, tranquil, and saying to me, "But you're after… well, here it is, this is it!"

So then, I understood why the mind and the vital were sent away from this body, and the psychic being was left (naturally, it was the psychic being that governed all movements earlier, so it was nothing new, but there were no more difficulties: all the complications coming from the vital and the mind, which add their imprints, their tendencies, it was all gone). So I understood: "Ah, that's it, it's this psychic being that is to become the supramental being."

I had never bothered to know what it looked like. But when I saw that, I understood. And I see it, I still see it, I have kept the memory. Its hair almost looked red, strangely (it wasn't like red hair, but it looked like it). And its expression! Such a fine expression, gently ironical... oh, extraordinary, extraordinary!

You understand, my eyes were open, it was an almost material vision.

Then one understands! All at once, all questions vanished, it became very clear, very simple.

(silence)

And the psychic is precisely what lives on. So if it materialized, it means doing away with death. But "doing away"... what's done away with is only what's not according to the Truth, that's what goes away—all that's incapable of being transformed in the image of the psychic, of being part of the psychic.

That's really interesting."

Chapter 19: The Gods Awake

The very first line of Savitri is "IT WAS the hour before the Gods awake.". In reading the last line of this same canto, "This was the day that Satyavan must die" one gets the sense that the Gods awakening is intimately related to the fact that Satyavan must die. For it is the human under the strong influence of the mind of Night, that dies, to allow a luminous Satyavan, the golden tower, the human who has reached full stature, to become the model of humanity.

Seeing differently, and holding within a different flame, that even allows the birth of the flame-child, a being that does not require sheaths of ignorance, but instead is cased in the safety of the supramental substance, would allow the Gods to awake.

Already we have seen Sri Aurobindo's reference to the 'future mighty Triad' in *Secret of the Veda*. Mother too speaks about different genres of gods. There are those from the Overmind world who engender habitual notions of morality, ethics, and religious feeling that are now outdated. The supramental world is already born and will progressively become more real allowing even a different genre of Gods, divine beings, who may choose to manifest when the supramental substance becomes material (CWM Vol 9, 10 July 1957, pp 148-152):

"It is quite difficult to free oneself from old habits of being and to be able to freely conceive of a new life, a new world. And naturally, the liberation begins on the highest planes of consciousness: it is easier for the mind or the higher intelligence to conceive of new things than for the vital being, for instance, to feel things in a new way. And it is still more difficult for the body to have a purely material perception of what a new world will be. Yet this perception must precede the material transformation; first one must feel very concretely the strangeness of the old things, their lack of relevance, if I may say so. One must have the feeling, even a material impression, that they are outdated, that they belong to a past which no longer has any purpose. For the old impressions one had of past things which have become historic—which have their interest from that point of view and support the advance of the present and the future—this is still a movement that belongs to the old world: it is the old world that is unfolding with a past, a present, a future. But for the creation of a new world, there is, so to speak, only a continuity of transition which gives an appearance—an impression rather—the impression of two things still intermingled but almost disconnected, and that the things of the past no longer have the power or the strength to endure, with whatever modifications, in the new things. That other world is necessarily an absolutely new experience. One would have to go back to the time when there was a transition from the animal to the human creation to find a similar period, and at that time the consciousness was not sufficiently mentalised to be able to observe, understand, feel intelligently—the passage must have been made in a completely obscure way. So, what I am speaking about is absolutely new, unique in the terrestrial creation, it is something unprecedented, truly a perception or a sensation or an impression... that is quite strange and new. (After a silence) A disconnection: something which has overstayed its time and has only quite a subordinate force of existence, from something totally new, but still so young, so imperceptible, almost weak, so to say; it hasn't yet the power to impose and assert itself and to predominate, to take the place of the other. So there is a concomitance but, as I said, with a disconnection, that is, the connection between the two is missing.

It is difficult to describe, but I am speaking to you about it because this is what I felt yesterday evening. I felt it so acutely... that it made me look at certain things, and once I had seen them I felt it would be interesting to tell you about them.

(Silence)

It seems strange that something so new, so special and I might say so unexpected should happen during a film-show. For people who believe that some things are important and other things are not, that there are activities which are helpful to yoga and others which are not, well, this is one more opportunity to show that they are wrong. I have always noticed that it is unexpected things which give you the most interesting experiences.

Yesterday evening, suddenly something happened which I have just described to you as best I could—I don't know if I have succeeded in making myself understood—but it was truly quite new and altogether unexpected. We were shown, comparatively clumsily, a picture of the temple on the banks of the Ganges, and the statue of Kali—for I suppose it was a photograph of that statue, I could not manage to get any precise information about it—and while I was seeing that, which was a completely superficial appearance and, as I said, rather clumsy, I saw the reality it was trying to represent, what was behind, and this put me in touch with all that world of religion and worship, of aspiration, man's whole relationship with the gods, which was—I am already speaking in the past tense—which was the flower of the human spiritual effort towards something more divine than man, something which was the highest and almost the purest expression of his effort towards what is higher than he. And suddenly I had concretely, materially, the impression that it was another world, a world that had ceased to be real, living, an outdated world which had lost its reality, its truth, which had been transcended, surpassed by something which had taken birth and was only beginning to express itself, but whose life was so intense, so true, so sublime, that all this became false, unreal, worthless.

Then I truly understood—for I understood not with the head, the intelligence but with the body, you understand what I mean—I understood in the cells of the body—that a new world is born and is beginning to grow.

And so, when I saw all this, I remembered something that had happened…. I think I remember rightly, in 1926.

Sri Aurobindo had given me charge of the outer work because he wanted to withdraw into concentration in order to hasten the manifestation of the supramental consciousness and he had announced to the few people who were there that he was entrusting to me the work of helping and guiding them, that I would remain in contact with him, naturally, and that through me he would do the work. Suddenly, immediately, things took a certain shape: a very brilliant creation was worked out in extraordinary detail, with marvellous experiences, contacts with divine beings, and all kinds of manifestations which are considered miraculous. Experiences followed one upon another, and, well, things were unfolding altogether brilliantly and… I must say, in an extremely interesting way.

One day, I went as usual to relate to Sri Aurobindo what had been happening—we had come to something really very interesting, and perhaps I showed a little enthusiasm in my account of what had taken place—then Sri Aurobindo looked at me… and said: "Yes, this is an Overmind creation. It is very interesting, very well done. You will perform miracles which will make you famous throughout the world, you will be able to turn all events on earth topsy-turvy, indeed,…" and then he smiled and said: "It will be a great success. But it is an Overmind creation. And it is not success that we want; we want to establish the Supermind on earth. One must know how to renounce immediate success in order to create the new world, the supramental world in its integrality."

With my inner consciousness I understood immediately: a few hours later the creation was gone… and from that moment we started anew on other bases.

Well, I announced to you all that this new world was born. But it has been so engulfed, as it were, in the old world that so far the difference has not been very perceptible to many people. Still, the action of the new forces has continued very regularly, very persistently, very steadily, and to a certain extent, very effectively. And one of the manifestations of this action was my experience—truly so very new—of yesterday evening. And the result of all this I have noted step by step in almost daily experiences. It could be expressed succinctly, in a rather linear way:

First, it is not only a "new conception" of spiritual life and the divine Reality. This conception was expressed by Sri Aurobindo, I have expressed it myself many a time, and it could be formulated somewhat like this: the old spirituality was an escape from life into the divine Reality, leaving the world just where it was, as it was; whereas our new vision, on the contrary, is a divinisation of life, a transformation of the material world into a divine world. This has been said, repeated, more or less understood, indeed it is the basic idea of what we want to do. But this could be a continuation with an improvement, a widening of the old world as it was—and so long as this is a conception up there in the field of thought, in fact it is hardly more than that—but what has happened, the really new thing, is that a new world is born, born, born. It is not the old one transforming itself, it is a new world which is born. And we are right in the midst of this period of transition where the two are entangled—where the other still persists all-powerful and entirely dominating the ordinary consciousness, but where the new one is quietly slipping in, still very modest, unnoticed—unnoticed to the extent that outwardly it doesn't disturb anything very much, for the time being, and that in the consciousness of most people it is even altogether imperceptible. And yet it is working, growing—until it is strong enough to assert itself visibly.

In any case, to simplify things, it could be said that characteristically the old world, the creation of what Sri Aurobindo calls the Overmind, was an age of the gods, and consequently the age of religions. As I said, the flower of human effort towards what is above it gave rise to innumerable religious forms, to a religious relationship between the best souls and the invisible world. And at the very summit of all that, as an effort towards a higher realisation there has arisen the idea of the unity of religions, of this "one single thing" which is behind all these manifestations; and this idea has truly been, so to speak, the extreme limit of human aspiration. Well, that is at the frontier, it is something that still belongs completely to the Overmind world, the Overmind creation and which from there seems to be looking towards this "other thing" which is a new creation it cannot grasp—which it tries to reach, feels coming, but cannot grasp. To grasp it, a reversal is needed. It is necessary to leave the Overmind creation. It was necessary that the new creation, the supramental creation should take place.

And now, all these old things seem so old, so out-of-date, so arbitrary—such a travesty of the real truth.

In the supramental creation there will no longer be any religions. The whole life will be the expression, the flowering into forms of the divine Unity manifesting in the world. And there will no longer be what men now call gods.

These great divine beings themselves will be able to participate in the new creation; but to do so, they will have to put on what we could call the "supramental substance" on earth. And if some of them choose to remain in their world as they are, if they decide not to manifest physically, their relation with the beings of a supramental earth will be a relation of friends, collaborators, equals, for the highest divine essence will be manifested in the beings of the new supramental world on earth.

When the physical substance is supramentalised, to incarnate on earth will no longer be a cause of inferiority, quite the contrary. It will give a plenitude which cannot be obtained otherwise.

But all this is in the future; it is a future... which has begun, but which will take some time to be realised integrally. Meanwhile we are in a very special situation, extremely special, without precedent. We are now witnessing the birth of a new world; it is very young, very weak—not in its essence but in its outer manifestation—not yet recognised, not even felt, denied by the majority. But it is here. It is here, making an effort to grow, absolutely sure of the result. But the road to it is a completely new road which has never before been traced out—nobody has gone there, nobody has done that! It is a beginning, a universal beginning. So, it is an absolutely unexpected and unpredictable adventure.

There are people who love adventure. It is these I call, and I tell them this: "I invite you to the great adventure."

It is not a question of repeating spiritually what others have done before us, for our adventure begins beyond that. It is a question of a new creation, entirely new, with all the unforeseen events, the risks, the hazards it entails—a real adventure, whose goal is certain victory, but the road to which is unknown and must be traced out step by step in the unexplored. Something that has never been in this present universe and that will never be again in the same way. If that interests you… well, let us embark. What will happen to you tomorrow—I have no idea.

One must put aside all that has been foreseen, all that has been devised, all that has been constructed, and then… set off walking into the unknown. And—come what may! There."

What is surprising though, is that even when 'The Spirit shall be the master of how world", still hostile forces shall exist:

"The Spirit shall be the master of his world
Lurking no more in form's obscurity
And Nature shall reverse her action's rule,
The outward world disclose the Truth it veils;
All things shall manifest the covert God,
All shall reveal the Spirit's light and might
And move to its destiny of felicity.

Even should a hostile force cling to its reign
And claim its right's perpetual sovereignty
And man refuse his high spiritual fate,
Yet shall the secret Truth in things prevail."
(Pg 708, *The Soul's Choice and the Supreme Consummation*, Book XI: *The Book of Everlasting Day*)

Perhaps this is also where the action of the 'future mighty Triad' becomes indispensable indicating the Gods who will awake. Recalling: "...Vishnu, Rudra, Brahmanaspati, the future mighty Triad, preside over the indispensable conditions, - for the one paces out the vast framework of the inner worlds in which our soul-action takes place, the other in his wrath and might and violent beneficence forces onward the great evolution and smites the opponent and the recusant and the ill-doer, and the third administers always the seed of the creative word from the profundities of the soul..." (pg 491, *The Secret of the Veda*).

For, 'the hour must come of the Transcendent's will' and the future mighty Triad must play a part in this:

"For in the march of all-fulfilling Time
The hour must come of the Transcendent's will:
All turns and winds towards his predestined ends
In Nature's fixed inevitable course
Decreed since the beginning of the worlds
In the deep essence of created things:
Even there shall come as a high crown of all
The end of Death, the death of Ignorance."
(Pg 708, The Soul's Choice and the Supreme Consummation, Book XI: The Book of Everlasting Day)

A few days after Mother's September 25, 1914 revelation, there is a related, revealing prayer in (CWM, Vol. 1: Prayers & Meditations, 1914, September 30) which Mother addresses the Lord, the Divine Mother, Agni, Indra, and Soma (whom she refers to as Sublime Love). This prayer may be illustrative of the Gods who will awake and is referred to only as an example of a larger phenomenon that only the Mother is privy to.

First, here is the prayer of September 25:

"The Lord has willed and Thou dost execute:
A new Light shall break upon the earth.
A new world shall be born,
And the things that were promised shall be fulfilled."

Here is the prayer of September 30:

"Lord, Thou hast broken down the barriers of thought and the realisation has appeared in all its amplitude. Not to forget any of its aspects, to carry out their accomplishment at the same time, without neglecting any of them, not to allow any limitation, any restriction to come in the way and delay our march, this is what Thou wilt help us to do through Thy supreme intervention. And all those who are Thyself, manifesting Thee in the perfection of some particular activity, will also be our collaborators, for such is Thy Will.

Our Divine Mother is with us and has promised us identification with the supreme and total consciousness—from the unfathomable depths to the most external world of the senses. And in all these domains Agni assures us of the help of his purifying flame, destroying all obstacles, kindling the energies, stimulating the will, so that the realisation may be hastened. Indra is with us for the perfection of the illumination in our knowledge; and the divine Soma has transformed us in his infinite, sovereign, marvellous love, bringer of the supreme beatitudes...

O divine and sweet Mother, I bow to Thee with a rapt, ineffable tenderness, and with infinite trust.

O splendid Agni, Thou who art so living within me, I call Thee, I invoke Thee that Thou mayst be more living still, that Thy brazier may become more immense, Thy flames higher and more powerful, that the entire being may now be only an ardent burning, a purifying pyre.

O Indra, I venerate and admire Thee, I implore Thee that Thou mayst unite with me, that Thou mayst definitively break down all the barriers of thought, that Thou mayst bestow upon me the divine knowledge.

O Thou, Sublime Love, to whom I gave never any other name, but who art so wholly the very substance of my being, Thou whom I feel vibrant and alive in the least of my atoms even as in the infinite universe and beyond, Thou who breathest in every breath, movest in the heart of all activities, art radiant through all that is of good will and hidden behind all sufferings, Thou for whom I cherish a cult without limit which grows ever more intense, permit that I may with more and more reason feel that I am Thyself wholly.

And Thou, O Lord, who art all this made one and much more, O sovereign Master, extreme limit of our thought, who standest for us at the threshold of the Unknown, make rise from that Unthinkable some new splendour, some possibility of a loftier and more integral realisation, that Thy work may be accomplished and the universe take one step farther towards the sublime Identity, the supreme Manifestation.

And now my pen falls mute and I adore Thee in silence."

The Lord has broken down the barriers of thought and there is a realization that appears in all its amplitude. There are helpers who manifest perfectly in some particular activities (and these may be the gods she addresses). But there are a few interesting things. First, Agni is in all the domains from the unfathomable depths to the external world of the senses, is also intimately in

Mother. Indra will provide perfection of the illumination of our knowledge, that also has to transcend the overmind planes. And she asks him to unite with her. And she refers to Soma as Sublime Love who is the very substance of her being, which again includes and transcends all known planes.

This likely implies a few things. First, if these gods can operate beyond the Overmind planes, then they must potentially be Gods. Second, if they are united with Mother, or do unite with her, they will likely materialize in supramental form. Finally, if the first and second are true, then perhaps these are amongst the Gods referred to in 'It was the hour before the Gods awake. This would be in addition to the Gods that will awake from the Unthinkable, that Mother refers to in addressing the Lord.

Chapter 20: High Truth's Feet

For the 'hour of the Transcendent's will', 'high Truth must first set her feet on earth' (Savitri, pg 708). What is this high Truth? Several passages in the *Agenda* refer to the presence of two realities, and how Mother experiences a frequent switching between the two. Staying in a reality of high Truth requires learning the mechanism of why the constant flipping or switching occurs.

The following is one such experience (Agenda, Vol. 08, 1967, September 20):

"Only an observation, which is really very interesting: it's that everyone has said the same thing, all those who have had the Experience have said the same thing ... but each one in his own way, so it looks like something different. Yesterday it was so clear, and again the whole morning, from early morning: this way, that way, this one here, that one there (Mother shows different facets), the philosophers, founders of religions, sages of all countries—they have always said the same thing. For instance, the Buddha's teaching and, say, the Christian teaching, seem to be so different, but it's always the same thing. That is to say, there is ONE state (if you catch hold of it), ONE state in which you are conscious of the divine Consciousness (not "conscious of": "conscious through" or "conscious with," I don't know how to explain ... it's the divine Consciousness which is conscious, that is, the Consciousness in its essence), and there are no more problems there, no more complications, no more explanations, nothing anymore—everything is as clear as can be. So then, each one has tried to explain that, and naturally it has become confused, incomplete, incorrect, with one explanation clashing with another—while everyone is talking about the same thing!

It came yesterday in relation to a boy who sent me the letter from one of his friends, in which he said the usual nonsense: "I don't believe in God because I can't see him." The usual little stupidity. And in that connection, I saw (I looked, like that, looked for a long time), I saw that the one who rejects, the one who asserts, the one ... all that, all of it is (how could I put it?) variations on the same theme, even when it appears to be saying the contrary.

Yesterday it was interesting, because the observation was the same for the materialists who feel that the only truth is a "concrete" truth, the truth that can, according to them, be seen or heard or touched.... And it's the same thing, the same state—the same state reflected in different mirrors. But the difference in mirrors is not an essential and radical difference, it's only ... (gesture showing facets in movement), yes, that's what some have called the "play," but it's not even a play; I could almost say it's a difference of position.

Everything you can say about it is nothing, it's part of that enormous jibbering that tries to express the inexpressible "something." But when you are IN it, it's so clear, so obvious—simple, without problems. And the world is no longer a problem.

Even that apparently rather fundamental difference between those who regard the Manifestation as divine and essential and those who consider that in order to reach the essential Divine you must leave the Manifestation (because it's an "error"—that is, an error that took place in the Consciousness), even those two positions are the same thing! But how can you explain it? When you say that, it seems foolish, yet up above it's true. It's true—true and full. It's full, not hollow—here everything rings hollow, so hollow; the hollowness of inadequacy. But up above...

It's almost like a kaleidoscope: you turn it and get one picture, turn it again and get another picture, turn it again ... yet it's always the same thing!

But now, it's the body that has the Experience. In a certain state, the state which corresponds to That, the essential state, everything is harmonious, with a living, smiling, happy peace; then as soon as there is ... a nothing, you know, a mere trifle, simply the coming into the atmosphere of something conflicting—a mere nothing—it's felt like something extremely acute and painful. But not in the way of the pain of Ignorance, it's more like ... you could call it an uneasiness, but it's not even that.... Everyone has explained it in his own way: some have called it "falling from the Truth into Falsehood," others "falling from the Light into Darkness," others "falling from Ananda into suffering," yet others ... Everyone has given his explanation, but it's something else.... As for me, I have no words for it, but the body feels it, feels it very acutely, and it sees that at the end of it, the consequence of it, is disintegration. And its whole effort is to strive to reestablish that inner harmony, that harmonic state in which everything becomes harmonious, everything—and in their appearance things haven't changed! Yet in one way they are marvellous, and in the other detestable.

The opposition between the two things is becoming more pronounced every minute: one moment everything is divine, the next moment everything is detestable—yet it's the same thing.

Since the 15th of August, since that experience at the balcony, it has become very clear.

But then, it has nothing to do with thought, or even with sensation: it's purely material (Mother touches the skin of her hands), and it's the difference between a progressive and unbroken harmony that has no reason to stop, which becomes more and more conscious, more and more harmonious, and also more and more ... we say blissful, happy and all that—but it's not that! It's "something" ... something SO NATURAL, so natural and... with the rhythm of eternity. So it is THAT, and then suddenly (gesture of reversal) you fall back into ... exactly the SAME THING, everything is the same, yet everything is the opposite!

To such an extent that you have a perception, a material perception, inexpressible because it's hardly mentalized, of a perfect Harmony which can, in the consciousness, turn into a serious illness! Things of that sort.

There is the vision, an extremely complex and at the same time complete vision, that those, for instance, who have tried to explain the power of imagination, of thought or will or faith (all those things: the direct action on matter), the vision that each of those things has caught hold of one little aspect of the Thing, but in the Thing, there are no divisions; it's something which, when you perceive or conceive it, is divided into scores of little things, but it's essentially ... (how should I put it?) a way of being, a state of consciousness—it's a WAY OF BEING, not even a "state of consciousness" because that implies "being conscious OF something" and it's not that: it's a way of being. And that way of being is what, in the human consciousness, expresses itself as "Ah, the Divine!"—by opposition, you understand. It's a PERFECTLY NATURAL and spontaneous way of being—but how, how does That become this? How does That become distorted?... You constantly, constantly (gesture as of tiny reversals) switch from one to the other, back and forth, over and over again, as if to learn—to learn how That becomes this (the mechanism of the passage). To us it looks like (to us, to all this poor consciousness that has gone through innumerable woeful experiences), it looks like a "relapse" into the old state; therefore it's not that. But what's the mechanism?...

In the end, we would have the solution only if we found the how and the why.

Constantly, constantly ... (same gesture of tiny reversals).

All the explanations people give are nothing but explanations. They are not THAT.

Knowing the why or the how probably implies the power to change everything….

In that case, it will come one day."

On Page 708 of *Savitri* the Supreme refers to all of man's members feeling the Spirit's touch, and the coming of a new life:

"But first high Truth must set her feet on earth
And man aspire to the Eternal's light
And all his members feel the Spirit's touch
And all his life obey an inner Force.
This too shall be; for a new life shall come,
A body of the Superconscient's truth,
A native field of Supernature's mights:
It shall make earth's nescient ground Truth's colony,
Make even the Ignorance a transparent robe
Through which shall shine the brilliant limbs of Truth
And Truth shall be a sun on Nature's head
And Truth shall be the guide of Nature's steps
And Truth shall gaze out of her nether deeps."
(Pg 708, *The Soul's Choice and the Supreme Consummation*, Book XI: *The Book of Everlasting Day*)

This passage gives the sense of the clear choice, one in which one can always flip back to 'high Truth', which will also strengthen Truth's hold to reinforce it being 'a sun on Nature's head', 'the guide of Nature's steps', and its 'gaze out of her nether deeps'.

The high Truth is being grounded more and more, and in *The Secret Knowledge* there is a revelatory passage about the superhuman Rider, and God growing up while the wise men talk and sleep.

First there is the Might maned with light that will change Time's course:

"Only the Immortals on their deathless heights
Dwelling beyond the walls of Time and Space,
Masters of living, free from the bonds of Thought,
Who are overseers of Fate and Chance and Will
And experts of the theorem of world-need,
Can see the Idea, the Might that change Time's course,
Come maned with light from undiscovered worlds,
Hear, while the world toils on with its deep blind heart,
The galloping hooves of the unforeseen event,
Bearing the superhuman Rider, near
And, impassive to earth's din and startled cry,
Return to the silence of the hills of God;
As lightning leaps, as thunder sweeps, they pass
And leave their mark on the trampled breast of Life."
(Pp 53-54, C IV: *The Secret Knowledge*, Bk I: *The Book of Beginnings*)

The world-creators listen with the patience of the Unborn to an unseen Truth:

"Above the world the world-creators stand,
In the phenomenon see its mystic source.
These heed not the deceiving outward play,
They turn not to the moment's busy tramp,
But listen with the still patience of the Unborn
For the slow footsteps of far Destiny
Approaching through huge distances of Time,
Unmarked by the eye that sees effect and cause,
Unheard mid the clamour of the human plane.
Attentive to an unseen Truth they seize
A sound as of invisible augur wings,
Voices of an unplumbed significance,
Mutterings that brood in the core of Matter's sleep."
(Pg 54, C IV: *The Secret Knowledge*, Bk I: *The Book of Beginnings*)

They guide the unheedful moving world to the Bliss for which its heart has cried:

"In the heart's profound audition they can catch
The murmurs lost by Life's uncaring ear,
A prophet-speech in Thought's omniscient trance.
Above the illusion of the hopes that pass,
Behind the appearance and the overt act,
Behind this clock-work Chance and vague surmise,
Amid the wrestle of force, the trampling feet,
Across the cries of anguish and of joy,
Across the triumph, fighting and despair,
They watch the Bliss for which earth's heart has cried
On the long road which cannot see its end
Winding undetected through the sceptic days
And to meet it guide the unheedful moving world."
(Pp 54-55, C IV: *The Secret Knowledge*, Bk I: *The Book of Beginnings*)

The earth will grow unexpectedly divine even as the masked Transcendent mounts his throne:

"Thus will the masked Transcendent mount his throne.
When darkness deepens strangling the earth's breast
And man's corporeal mind is the only lamp,
As a thief's in the night shall be the covert tread
Of one who steps unseen into his house.
A Voice ill-heard shall speak, the soul obey,
A Power into mind's inner chamber steal,
A charm and sweetness open life's closed doors
And beauty conquer the resisting world,
The Truth-Light capture Nature by surprise,
A stealth of God compel the heart to bliss
And earth grow unexpectedly divine."
(Pg 55, C IV: *The Secret Knowledge*, Bk I: *The Book of Beginnings*)

God shall grow up, and belief shall be not till the work is done:

In Matter shall be lit the spirit's glow,

In body and body kindled the sacred birth;
Night shall awake to the anthem of the stars,
The days become a happy pilgrim march,
Our will a force of the Eternal's power,
And thought the rays of a spiritual sun.
A few shall see what none yet understands;
God shall grow up while the wise men talk and sleep;
For man shall not know the coming till its hour
And belief shall be not till the work is done."
(Pg 55, C IV: *The Secret Knowledge*, Bk I: *The Book of Beginnings*)

The work goes on, silently. Satyavan, the soul of the earth, the golden tower, holds new statuses animated by the flame-child to stabilize intermediate races, until Sri Aurobindo himself arrives in the first supramental body built in the supramental way, engendering even brighter rays in Savitri's continuing Dawn.

A Contemplative Map of Earth's Evolution

www.ingramcontent.com/pod-product-compliance
Lightning Source LLC
Chambersburg PA
CBHW071509040426
42444CB00008B/1559